Marie Louise,
the Island of Elba,
and the Hundred Days

Maria Luigia

Marie Louise

THE ISLAND OF ELBA, AND THE HUNDRED DAYS

BY

IMBERT DE SAINT-AMAND

TRANSLATED BY

ELIZABETH GILBERT MARTIN

WITH PORTRAIT

WILDSIDE PRESS

MANHATTAN PRESS
474 W. BROADWAY
NEW YORK

CONTENTS.

CHAPTER PAGE

 I. THE RETURN OF MARIE LOUISE TO AUSTRIA........ 1

 II. NAPOLEON'S ARRIVAL AT THE ISLAND OF ELBA..... 11

 III. QUEEN MARIE CAROLINE 22

 IV. MARIE LOUISE AT AIX IN SAVOY.................. 31

 V. MARIE LOUISE IN SWITZERLAND.................... 46

 VI. MARIE LOUISE DURING THE CONGRESS OF VIENNA... 54

 VII. THE RETURN FROM ELBA.......................... 82

 VIII. MARIE LOUISE DURING THE HUNDRED DAYS........ 111

 IX. THE FIELD OF MAY.............................. 138

 X. WATERLOO 155

 XI. NAPOLEON II................................... 172

 XII. MALMAISON.................................... 200

 XIII. ROCHEFORT................................... 214

 XIV. THE BELLEROPHON............................... 238

 XV. THE NORTHUMBERLAND............................ 260

MARIE LOUISE,

THE ISLAND OF ELBA, AND THE HUNDRED DAYS.

I.

THE RETURN OF MARIE LOUISE TO AUSTRIA.

FROM the double point of view of psychology and history it is a sad but curious task to study the gradations by which the Empress Marie Louise was, little by little, transformed from a devoted and irreproachable wife into a forgetful, indifferent, and faithless one. When she left the soil of France, her sentiments toward her husband were still honest. If she had not rejoined him at Fontainebleau, the fault should be attributed to him rather than to her. To the very end she had fulfilled her duties as Regent with exactness and loyalty, and Napoleon rendered her entire justice on this point. We believe that, when she entered Switzerland, she was still minded to go to Elba very soon. During the early days of her sojourn at Schoenbrunn she remained more French than Austrian. She greatly preferred the Duchess of Montebello to any of the Viennese court ladies; she showed high esteem for Madame de Montesquiou, M.

1

de Bausset, and M. de Méneval, who constantly talked to her of Napoleon and of France; she retained her husband's imperial coat-of-arms upon her carriages, her silver, and the liveries of her attendants. Her household was entirely French, and at the court of her father she was reproached with always playing the part of Empress. The Countess of Montesquiou, who continued to fulfil her functions as governess with the greatest zeal, talked unceasingly of the Emperor Napoleon to the little Bonaparte, as the unfortunate King of Rome was styled at Vienna. She taught the child to love his father and to pray for him.

The Emperor Francis proceeded slowly and by degrees. He was too adroit to precipitate counsels or commands which at the first moment his daughter might have found cynical. He did nothing to wound or shock her. He permitted her to take the waters at Aix-les-Bains, which, in 1814, was still a French town, and where she went out driving in open carriages bearing the imperial arms of France.

At this time the attitude of Marie Louise was still absolutely correct. But the crafty Austrian policy understood how to find a man who should succeed in turning the wife from her husband. This man was a military diplomatist, General Count Neipperg, a relentless enemy of France and of Napoleon. Complaisant, skilful, energetic, a thorough man of the world, an accomplished courtier, an excellent musician, he knew how to make his way by insinuation as well as by force. He was married to a divorced woman whom he had abducted from her husband, who was still living in 1814, and by whom he had several children. He had but one eye, having lost the other in battle, and he wore a black bandage to hide the scar. He might have been the father of Marie Louise, for he was by twenty-one years her senior. Who could have imagined that this man would be the successor of the Emperor Napoleon? General Neipperg, as husband of the Empress Marie Louise, is not less astonishing than the Widow Scarron, the spouse of the Sun-King. In history we pass from one surprise to another, and find in destiny a fantastic something which causes the life of peoples as well as of individuals to seem like a dream.

After the abdication at Fontainebleau, Napoleon was not yet, in appearance at least, on ill terms with his father-in-law. On April 16, 1814, the Emperor Francis had written him thus, from Rambouillet: —

"MONSIEUR MY BROTHER AND DEAR SON-IN-LAW: The tender solicitude which I feel toward the Empress, my daughter, has induced me to meet her here. I arrivèd only a few hours ago, and I am but too well convinced that her health has suffered extremely since I saw her last. I have decided to propose her return to the bosom of her family for some months. She is in the greatest need of calm and repose, and Your Majesty has given her too many proofs of veritable attachment, for me to doubt that you will consent to my wishes and approve my determination.   When she is restored to health, my daughter will take possession of her territory, which will quite naturally bring her nearer to the abode of Your Majesty.   Doubtless it would be superfluous for me to give Your Majesty the assurance that your son will form a part of my family, and that, during his residence in my dominions, I shall share the solicitude owed him by his mother.   Receive, Monsieur my brother, the assurance of my most distinguished consideration.   I am Your Imperial Majesty's attached brother and father-in-law,   FRANCIS."

But it was not this letter that expressed the real sentiments of the Emperor of Austria; these were contained in the one he had written five days earlier to Prince Metternich, in which these significant lines occur: "The important thing is to get Napoleon away from France; and God grant he may be sent very far!   You were right not to defer the conclusion of the treaty until I should arrive in Paris, for it is only by this means that an end can be put to the war. I do not approve the choice of the Island of Elba as a residence for Napoleon; they take it from Tuscany; they dispose of things which properly belong to my family in favor of foreigners.   This must not occur again.   Besides, Napoleon remains too close to France and to Europe.   However, if the thing cannot be prevented, we must try to secure that Elba revert to Tuscany after Napoleon's death; that I be named co-guardian of the child for Parma; and that, in case of the death of my daughter and the child, the territory destined for them be not retained for the family of Napoleon."

It is more than evident that the Emperor Francis, even admitting that he had ever had any sympathy with his son-in-law, which is doubtful, no longer retained the slightest trace of it. He thought him a danger to Europe in general, and to Austria in particular. Napoleon still preserved his illusions; he imagined that his father-in-law was seriously interested in his fate and had obtained for him the sovereignty of the Island of Elba, poor flotsam from a colossal shipwreck. Napoleon deceived himself. For the Island of Elba he was indebted solely to the magnanimity of the Emperor Alexander, whom he had injured so deeply, and who behaved like a generous enemy. The Austrian, on the contrary, showed himself implacable towards the man to whom he had pardoned neither Wagram nor Marengo.

On May 2, 1814, Marie Louise left France. Escorted by a detachment of Swiss cavalry, which received her at the frontier, she entered Basle the same day between a double row of Swiss, Austrian, and Bavarian troops. Her suite and that of her son was composed of the Countess of Montesquiou, who still retained her post as governess to the little Prince; the Duchess of Montebello, who, although not a lady-of-honor, had wished to accompany the Empress as far as Vienna, in order to delay for a few days a separation which was painful to them both; the Countess of Brignole, who had succeeded Madame de Montebello, and who was to remain with and die in the service of Marie Louise; General Cafarelli; Baron de Saint-Aignan; Doctor Corvisart, the surgeon Lacorner, who intended to return to France in a few days with the Duchess of Montebello; Baron de Méneval; Madame Hureau de Sorbec; Baron de Bausset, Madame Rabusson, and Madame Soufflot, who expected to remain for several years longer in attendance on the Empress. Nothing that concerned her personal service was changed. She retained the same individuals, the same display, the same customs, the same household arrangements, the same etiquette, the same domestics, the same equipages. Her retinue occupied twenty-four carriages. The expenses of the journey across France amounted to fifty thousand francs. Marie Louise travelled as a sovereign; and yet the little King of Rome perceived a change in his destiny. "Ah!" said he, "I see very well I am no longer a king, for I have no longer any pages."

At Basle, Marie Louise received a letter which Napoleon had addressed to her from Fréjus, on April 28, 1814; it revived in her heart the regret she had often expressed for not having gone to meet her husband at Fontainebleau. M. de Méneval also received a letter, dated at Fréjus, in which General Bertrand said to him: "We had a sad journey, as you can easily believe; good enough through nearly the whole of France, where the Emperor received testimonies of regret, and the respect due to his position; but in Provence we were exposed to in-

sults which, happily, have not been repeated. You
must be aware how greatly we desire that the Empress should divide her time between Parma and
the Island of Elba; we should be so happy to see
her now and then. She has been so kind to my wife
and me that I desire this more keenly than any one.
I beg you to lay at her feet the homage of my
respectful devotion. The Emperor continues in good
health, notwithstanding the cruel position in which
he has been placed for the last month."

At this moment the ties which attached Marie
Louise to Napoleon were not broken. We desire
no other proof of it than this long letter which she
wrote to her father from Zurich: "At Basle I had
the consolation of receiving news from the Emperor.
He is well, but he is very much pained by the manner
in which he was received in Provence. He has also
other anxieties about which I wish to consult you.
You know how disagreeable it is to me to speak of
money. But I think it my duty, as wife and mother,
to explain to you the condition in which the Emperor
has been placed, and to beg your intervention. I do
not ask anything for myself, because I believe that
if I were in need, you would not let me want for
anything. The Emperor has very little money with
him. Ten or twelve millions, the fruit of his econo-
mies on the civil list for twelve years, and a great
number of snuff-boxes set round with brilliants, are
at Orléans, confiscated unlawfully by a commissary
of the Provisional Government. All this belongs to

the Emperor and my son. They have even carried
off his library and other things which he used daily.
I entreat you to employ all possible means that he
may be put in possession of what is his. Things
which belonged to the crown — diamonds, bank de-
posits, and other papers — have been returned through
the intermediary of the directors or treasurers. The
Emperor has been credited on the civil list with an
annuity of two millions; but the manner in which
the government is acting does not permit the hope
that it will ever be paid, unless you, my dear father,
whose character is so just, defend the interests of
your son-in-law, who is no longer your enemy. My
absolute confidence in your generosity and your
goodness induces me to make this application. I am
sure that my confidence will not be deceived."

While Marie Louise, still faithful to her duties,
thus pleaded the cause of her husband, the Austrian
oligarchy was seeking every possible means to make
their separation final. Nothing was left undone
which could give the return of the dethroned sovereign to her own country the appearance of a victory
rather than a defeat. Marie Louise was received
everywhere with the same eclat, the same respect,
the same splendor as in the palace of the Tuileries.
" Our journey," said Baron de Bausset, who was one
of her suite, " was more like a triumph than a festi-
val; one might justly have thought that Austria,
obliged for a time to part with an adored princess,
celebrated her return as a conquest. The sovereigns

of Baden, Würtemberg, and Bavaria, whose extreme
frontiers we crossed, sent deputations of the highest
crown officials to meet her; nothing was lacking but
triumphal arches to make one believe that we were
on the faithful and submissive soil of the old Confederation of the Rhine. After having admired the
famous falls of the Rhine, near Schaffhausen, and
the beautiful lakes of Zurich and Constance, we
arrived at the Tyrol." There the people saluted the
august traveller with transports of joy and enthusiasm which verged on frenzy.

The Tyrol, which Napoleon had annexed to Bavaria
against the wishes of its inhabitants, still belonged
to that power, but in a few weeks it was to be restored to Austria. The Tyrolese considered the passage of Marie Louise an occasion for displaying their
sentiments of affection and loyalty to the Hapsburg
dynasty. At Fuessen, Reutte, Innspruck, and Salzburg the excitement was general. Snow fell in vain.
Nothing could chill the people's enthusiasm. These
brave and loyal Tyrolese, whom Alfred de Musset
has described as

> " a people heroic and proud,
> Mountaineers like the eagle, and free like the air,"

celebrated the arrival of the daughter of the Austrian
Emperor as a signal of deliverance. They unhar-
nessed the horses from her carriage and that of her
son, and drew them with their own hands. All along
the route fireworks were set off to the flourish of

trumpets, responded to by troops of singers so placed that their voices sounded like distant echoes. The towns were illuminated. At every chateau where the wife and son of Napoleon reposed, Tyrolese in yellow hats adorned with green feathers mounted guard. Never did sovereign receive a warmer welcome.

After leaving Salzburg, Marie Louise journeyed towards Vienna by the way of Moelk. At the abbey of this name she found Prince Trautmansdorff, chief equerry, who had been despatched by the Empress of Austria, to inquire at what hour in the morning she would leave there. Four leagues from Vienna, between Saint Poelten and Siegartskirchen, she met her step-mother, the Empress of Austria, who had come to bid her welcome, and who was accompanied by Countess Lazanski, who had been grand mistress of the household to Marie Louise until her marriage. When the carriages came together, the Empress of Austria resigned hers to the Duchess of Montebello and Countess Lazanski, and entered that of her step-daughter. On the same evening, May 18, 1814, Marie Louise arrived at the Castle of Schoenbrunn, the end of her journey. She was received there by the arch-dukes, her brothers, and her uncles. Her sisters, who were waiting for her at the door of her apartments, threw their arms about her, and felicitated her on her return as if it were a happy miracle. And, beholding once more the places where her infancy had been spent, the former Empress of the French felt all her German patriotism reawaken in her soul.

II.

MARIE LOUISE crossed the frontier of France for the last time, May 2, 1814. On the following day Napoleon reached Elba on the English frigate *Undaunted*. He had not been free from disquieting thoughts concerning his probable reception there. Would the French garrison, commanded by General Dalesme, the governor of the island, deliver up to him the territory they guarded? Among the islanders there were some who wished to be called English; others who desired to be free from any master. On several promontories might be seen floating, almost side by side, the white flag and the tricolor.

Toward nightfall on May 3 the *Undaunted* neared Porto-Ferrajo and hove to about a quarter of a league from the town. A few minutes later she put off a small boat containing General Drouot, the Emperor's commissary, Count Klamm, and Lieutenant Smith. They were the bearers of an order from the French government, directing General Dalesme to deliver his command to General Drouot, together with the island, the forts, and all munitions of war. The

11

latter, on landing, received from General Dalesme the keys of the town, the forts, and three hundred and twenty-five cannon.

This accomplished, General Dalesme went on board the English frigate, accompanied by all the local authorities, who were anxious to present themselves to their new sovereign. Napoleon questioned them concerning the island and its inhabitants and then dismissed them, after having ordered the sub-prefect to convoke the mayors and the parish priests. The population of Porto-Ferrajo, convinced that the Emperor had brought great treasures with him, had already assembled in the public square, and were impatiently awaiting their illustrious monarch. But at eleven o'clock, Napoleon, having tacked about the island, caused General Dalesme to be informed that his formal entry would be deferred to the afternoon of May 4.

On the morning of that day the following proclamation of General Dalesme was found posted on the walls of Porto-Ferrajo: —

"Inhabitants of the island of Elba: the vicissitudes natural to humanity have brought the Emperor Napoleon hither; his choice has given him to you as sovereign. Before entering these walls, your new and august monarch addressed to me the following words, which I hasten to make known to you, because they are the pledge of your future happiness: 'General, I have sacrificed my rights to the interests of my country, reserving to myself, with the consent of all the Powers, the sovereignty and ownership of the Island of Elba. Be so good as to make the people acquainted with the new state of affairs, and the choice I have made of their island for my residence; I have selected it on account of the mildness of their manners and their climate. Tell them that they will always be the object of my most lively interest.' — Elbans! there is no need of comment on these words. They fix your destiny. The Emperor has judged you rightly. I owe you this justice, and I render it. People of Elba, I shall soon leave you. My departure will pain me, for I love you sincerely; but the thought of your happiness will sweeten my sorrow, and in whatever place I may be I shall remain near this island in spirit, through my memory of the virtues of its inhabitants and the wishes I shall form for them."

By noon the troops were under arms, and the authorities assembled at the wharf. The Emperor's landing at three o'clock was announced by a salute of twenty-one guns from the English frigate and as many from the guns of the fortress. Napoleon was at once harangued by the authorities of the island, and he responded very nearly in these words : —

" The mildness of your climate, and the romantic scenery of your island, have decided me to choose it, among all my vast domains, for the place of my abode. I hope that you will know how to appreciate this preference, and that you will love me like submissive children; you will then find me always disposed to have for you the solicitude of a father."

As soon as Napoleon had finished this little speech, three violinists and two violoncellists who accompanied the Elban officials began to play; the Emperor placed himself under a canopy, and was conducted in procession to the church, where the *Te Deum* was intoned. Strange irony of fate — the fallen sovereign of an immense empire causing the *Te Deum* to be chanted because he has lost all his dominions except the Island of Elba!

The ceremony ended, Napoleon went to the town hall, where he was to lodge. The hall which was ordinarily used for public balls had been ornamented with a few little pictures and some chandeliers. In the middle of it a throne had been hastily erected, and decorated with gilded paper and fragments of scarlet cloth. Many of the crowd that followed the sovereign were allowed to enter. He urged the mayors to maintain order in their communes, and the pastors to preach concord among their flocks. Then the new colors were hoisted, as we learn from the subjoined official report: —

"To-day, May 4, 1814, His Majesty the Emperor Napoleon, having taken possession of the Island of Elba, General Drouot, governor of the island in the name of the Emperor, raised the new flag above the forts; a white ground crossed diagonally with a red band sown with three bees upon a ground of gold. This standard was saluted by the batteries of the coast forts, the English frigate *Undaunted*, and the French men-of-war which were in the harbor. In witness whereof, we, commissioners of the Allied Powers, together with General Drouot and General Dalesme, have signed this report."

The next morning Napoleon went out on foot at five o'clock to visit all the public institutions. He did not come in until nine o'clock, having overwhelmed with questions every one he met. He commanded various alterations. He would have liked to transform the barracks of Saint Francis at once into a palace wherein he might take up his residence. On May 6, he started very early to go and see the mines at Rio. He examined everything with scrupulous attention, and gave great praise to the director of the mines. He was occupying himself as diligently with an island twenty leagues in circumference and containing twelve thousand inhabitants, as he had done with the gigantic empire which extended from Rome to Dantzic. The same day, with a view to gaining the affections of the Elbans, he contributed sixty thousand francs toward the construction of roads long contemplated, but never begun for want of funds. He possessed this sum in uncoined gold, and he had it minted, in order that his generosity might produce a greater effect when his servants carried it in sacks across the town. Nobody talked of anything but his immense treasures and the prodigies he was going to perform. The people were enthusiastic for their new sovereign: he inflamed their southern imaginations.

On May 6, the Vicar-General Arrighi issued a charge which resembles a hymn of thanksgiving: —

"To my well-beloved in the Lord, my brethren of the clergy, and all the faithful of the island, health and benediction. Divine Providence, which in its benevolence irresistibly disposes all things, and assigns their destinies to nations, has willed that in the midst of the political changes of Europe, we should become for the future the subjects of Napoleon the Great. The Island of Elba, already celebrated for its natural productions, will hereafter become illustrious in the history of nations by the homage it renders to its new Prince, whose glory is immortal. The Island of Elba, in fact, takes rank among nations, and its narrow territory is ennobled by the name of its sovereign. Raised to so sublime an honor, it receives in its bosom the *Anointed of the Lord,* and the other distinguished personages who accompany him. . . . What wealth is about to inundate our country! What multitudes will hasten from all parts to gaze upon the hero! The first day that he set foot upon this shore he proclaimed our destiny and our happiness. '*I will be a good father,*' said he; '*be my beloved children.*' Dear Catholics, what words of tenderness! What expressions of good-will! What a pledge of your future felicity! May these words charm your thoughts delightfully and be strongly imprinted in your souls; they will prove an inexhaustible source of consolation!"

Never had Napoleon been more lauded in the days of his greatest splendor. May 7, he removed to the building intended for the military engineers, ceding to its officers, until they should depart, the rooms he had occupied at the town-hall. The building was only one story high, with six front windows; but it was isolated, had a pretty garden, and commanded views of the city and the sea. From among the citizens he chose four chamberlains, giving them salaries of twelve hundred francs; three orderlies; and two stewards of the palace. This little court of Porto-Ferrajo bore small resemblance to the splendid court of the Tuileries.

The Emperor announced that he would receive ladies twice a week, at eight o'clock in the evening, and they accepted this flattering invitation. Napoleon made his appearance among them, and asked each the name and profession of her husband. Most of them replied that they were engaged in commerce. The Emperor desired to know what branch of commerce. One was a baker; another a butcher; and so on. Chateaubriand says: "Bonaparte was continually returning throughout his life, to the two sources whence it sprang, democracy and royal power. His power came to him from the masses of the people; his rank from his genius. So one sees him pass without effort from the public square to the throne; from the kings and queens who thronged about him at Erfurt, to the butchers and oil-sellers who danced in his grange at Porto-Ferrajo."

From the 7th of May to the 25th, the Emperor busied himself with the repairs on his house, and in fencing the approaches to it. He superintended the work himself; by five o'clock in the morning he was among the masons in buckles and silk stockings. On May 25, arrived the frigate *Dryade*, commanded by Vicomte de Moncabrié, and the brig *Inconstant*, commanded by Vicomte de Charrier-Moissard. The frigate was to take back the French garrison from the island, and the brig to remain for Napoleon.

Before the departure from Fontainebleau, General Drouot had chosen for the Emperor among the Old Guard, all of them ready to follow their sovereign, something like six hundred grenadiers and foot-soldiers, one hundred cavalry-men, and a score or so of marines; in all, seven hundred and eighty picked men. Having marched from Fontainebleau to Savona, these brave and faithful soldiers embarked on five English transports, and landed at Porto-Ferrajo, in the night of May 25–26, 1814. Their arrival caused Napoleon great joy. At the sight of them he felt all his ambition and military ardor rekindle. Chateaubriand, in his *Mémoires d'outre-tombe*, has remarked: "The Allied Powers felicitated themselves on having left him, in derision as it were, a few hundred soldiers; he needed no more than that to summon all Europe once more to arms." To his little band the Emperor added sixty Poles whom he sent for from Parma; moreover, just as the two French battalions of the 35th Light Infantry were about to take ship for France, he announced that he would keep with him as many as, having been released from military service, would consent to enroll themselves under his flag. He managed in this way to retain about three hundred, nearly all Corsicans. He further added some three hundred Elbans to his little army, and thus found himself at the head of fifteen hundred soldiers. He organized a vigilant police throughout the island and made an excellent place of Porto-Ferrajo. The town was no longer recognizable. Workmen of all trades established themselves there. Foreigners flocked in, drawn either by curiosity or the hope of speculating to advantage. The price of all wares doubled; rents rose to extravagant figures. General Bertrand wrote, May 27, 1814, to M. de Méneval: "The Emperor is very happy here, and seems to have entirely forgotten how differently he was situated a short time ago. He is very busy adorning and furnishing his house, and in finding a site for a country-seat. We often speak of our excellent Empress." And again, June 25: "We learn from the newspapers that the Empress has arrived at Vienna. The Emperor continues well. We go about a good deal on horseback, as well as in boats and carriages. The Emperor's dwelling is already much improved, and others are being arranged in various places throughout the island. We hope soon to receive news from the Empress and the Prince her son."

Napoleon was still under the delusion that his wife and son would rejoin him at Elba in a few weeks, and this hope delighted him. On June 26, the imperial guard gave an entertainment to the inhabitants.

There was a ball, at which the Emperor made his appearance, and walked about the room, chatting with and questioning the ladies, as he had done at the Tuileries.

On the whole, the time which Napoleon passed at Elba was not unhappy. After so many emotions, he needed some repose. A delightful climate, the sea-views, the language of the people, which was his mother tongue, the battalions of his Old Guard, the fanatical devotion of his attendants, who were ready to shed the last drop of their blood for him, — all this was not without charm. He gave his little island the same solicitous care that he had given his immense empire. Does not a captain occupy himself with his company as fully as a commander-in-chief with his army? The interest one takes in things is not measured by their importance. A laborer often loves his thatched hut more than a sovereign does his palace. Napoleon regarded himself as spending the season at Elba, so to say, and had a presentiment that some day or other he would leave it. Moreover, he experienced a malicious pleasure in following attentively the mistakes the Bourbons were making; and to read the French journals gave him infinite joy. It was all very well for him to say, as he sometimes did, that, as a philosopher weaned from human grandeur, he wished to live hereafter like a justice of the peace in an English shire. But one morning, when, on climbing a knoll which overlooks Porto-Ferrajo, he beheld the sea breaking at the foot of the cliffs on every side, he could not refrain from exclaiming, " The devil ! It must be owned, my island is small enough ! "

At bottom he was tired neither of war nor of glory; and the ambitious sovereign of the Island of Elba, in his pretended retreat, resembled neither Diocletian in the gardens of Salona, nor Unarles Fifth in the convent of Saint-Just.

III.

WHILE Napoleon was getting settled on the Island of Elba, Marie Louise was resuming, at Schoenbrunn, the habits of her childhood and early youth. The life she led in this peaceful retreat must have been agreeable after so many tumults. Her mornings were devoted to her son, whose apartment communicated with her own, through a dressing-room. During the day, she drew, practised music, and studied Italian, a language she would need at Parma; she rode; she walked or drove in the park of Schoenbrunn or its suburbs; she visited the curiosities of Vienna. Silent and respectful crowds always showed themselves eager to see her; and the beauty of her son, who was the most charming child in the world, excited general admiration. She took great pleasure in the company of her young sisters: Leopoldine, born in 1797 (future Empress of Brazil); Marie Clementine, born in 1798 (future Princess of Salerno); Caroline Ferdinande, born in 1801 (future Princess of Saxe); Marie Anne, born in 1804 (future Abbess of the Chapter of the Noble Ladies of Prague).

22

She saw her brothers very often also : Ferdinand, the Prince Imperial, born in 1793; and Francis Charles Joseph, born in 1802. This Prince, who was the father of the present Emperor of Austria, was the playmate of the King of Rome, now called the Prince of Parma.

The saddle and carriage horses, state carriages, and wagons laden with the private property of Marie Louise, which had left Rambouillet under the escort of Austrian troops, reached Vienna in June. Among the saddle horses was an Arabian which had been Napoleon's favorite mount. Some one proposed that the Emperor of Austria should use it when he made his ceremonious entry into Vienna, but he had the good taste to decline this sort of triumph.

Marie Louise was awaiting her father with impatience. She had seen him last at Rambouillet, and in him were centred all her hopes. Early in the morning of June 15, 1814, she left Schoenbrunn to meet him. She stopped at Siegartskirchen, two leagues from Vienna. She had been preceded by her brothers and sisters and her step-mother. She received her father at the station, in the same room where Napoleon, in 1805, had received the deputation which brought him the keys of Vienna. The Emperor Francis got into his daughter's carriage, and went with her to Schoenbrunn. He left her under no illusions concerning the kind of protection he meant to give her. " As my daughter," he said frankly, "all that I have. is yours; as a sovereign I do not know you." The next day he made his triumphal entry into his capital, where he had not been since the last war. He passed through all its streets amidst joyful acclamations. The procession lasted five hours, and ended at the cathedral of Saint Stephen, where a *Te Deum* was intoned. Then the Emperor returned to Schoenbrunn with Marie Louise.

The entire family of the former Empress of the French conspired to alienate her from her husband. There was but one among her relatives who sought to recall her to sentiments of duty. This was her grandmother, Marie Caroline, the Queen of the Two Sicilies, who had but just arrived at Vienna. She was the daughter of the great Empress Maria Theresa, and the sister of Marie Antoinette, the unfortunate Queen of France. Prolific, like her illustrious mother, she had borne eighteen children, among whom was Marie Thérèse, the second wife of the Emperor Francis and the mother of the Empress Marie Louise. The life of Queen Marie Caroline had been full of vicissitudes. Courageous to heroism, energetic to cruelty, religious to superstition, autocratic to despotism, her existence was crowded with revolutions, troubles, and crises of every description. Born August 8, 1752, she married, on April 7, 1768, Ferdinand IV., King of the Two Sicilies, who began to reign in 1759. In 1800 she came to Vienna, to be near her daughter and her son-in-law. She remained two years, seeking with all her might to augment, if that were possible, the hatred felt towards France and French ideas by the court, the aristocracy, and the whole Austrian people.

When she heard of Bonaparte's victory at Marengo, Marie Caroline lost consciousness, and nearly died of apoplexy. She detested France as heartily as she did Napoleon. The Revolution had slain her sister, and the Empire had robbed her of the throne of Naples. There was one man, however, for whom her aversion was even greater than for Napoleon. She was probably the first to perceive, in 1813, that Murat was inclined to abandon France, and seek an alliance with Austria. She was then reigning with her husband in Sicily, under the domination of the English, whom she regarded rather as tyrants than as protectors. At this time she was half inclined to seek a reconciliation with Napoleon, and she sent an agent to Vienna to warn the French ambassador of the approaching defection of Murat.

In 1814 there were, singularly enough, two queens of the Two Sicilies, each of them named Caroline — one the sister of Marie Antoinette, the other the sister of Napoleon; and at this epoch, the most Napoleonic of the two was not Murat's wife. Nor is it less strange that, when these two women were struggling with equal fury for the throne of Naples, Prince Metternich was far more favorable to Caroline the sister of Napoleon, than to Caroline the Hapsburg, who had been the mother-in-law of his sovereign, the Emperor of Austria. The monarch of Elba must have been more than a little surprised if he learned

who it was that befriended him with most energy,
and was alone in exhorting his wife to remain faithful
to her conjugal duty.

Marie Louise remembered having seen her grandmother when she was a child, and was glad to meet
her again. The old Queen's journey had been a
veritable adventure. Accompanied by a few faithful attendants, she had stolen away from Sicily,
which her hatred of the British domination made
her consider as a prison. So fearful was she of being arrested by one or other of the English vessels
crowding the harbors of Malta and the Adriatic, that
she hastened through the Archipelago and never
stopped until she reached Constantinople. After
resting there a few days, she crossed the Bosphorus,
entered the Black Sea, and landed at Odessa after a
long and perilous voyage. From there she went to
Vienna, proposing to employ every means in her
power to dethrone Murat and repossess herself of
the Kingdom of Naples.

Queen Marie Caroline installed herself in the little
castle of Hetzendorf, which communicated by an
avenue with the park of Schoenbrunn. She saw
Marie Louise and the little King of Rome, her great-
grandchild, constantly. Not only did she show extreme affection for them both, but she was very
gracious to all the French who made part of the
household of Marie Louise. Baron de Méneval says
of Marie Caroline: "This Princess, who had been
Napoleon's declared enemy during the time of his

prosperity, and whose opinion could not be suspected
of partiality, professed a high esteem for his great
qualities. Learning that I had been his secretary,
she sought occasions to talk with me about him.
She said he had formerly given her great reason to
complain; that he had wounded her pride ('for I
was fifteen years younger, then,' she added); but
that now, since he was unfortunate, she had forgotten all. She could not restrain her indignation at
the manœuvres by which they were trying to detach
her grandchild from the ties which were her glory,
and thus deprive the Emperor of the sweetest consolation he could receive after the immense sacrifices
exacted from his pride. She added that if their reunion was forbidden, Marie Louise should tie her
sheets to the window and escape in disguise. 'That
is what I would do in her place,' said she; 'for when
one is married, it is for life.'"

After quoting these words, M. de Méneval goes on
to say: "But such a bold act, which would have had
an attraction for the daring spirit of the old Queen,
agreed neither with the character of Marie Louise,
nor with her ideas of decorum. Besides, she had
begun to be pleased with the thought of going presently to Parma, where she would be her own mistress and free to go and come as she chose." At
this time, however, she was not yet under the influence of Count Neipperg; and as she had not given
up the idea of going to visit Napoleon now and then
at Elba, she listened with a certain sympathy to the

counsels of her grandmother concerning conjugal fidelity.

Baron de Bausset observes that there was at this moment a likeness between the positions of these two dethroned sovereigns, one of whom was claiming the Duchy of Parma and the other the Kingdom of Naples. More vivacious and ardent than her granddaughter, Marie Caroline seemed greatly irritated by the legal obstructions put in her way by all the Powers, not excepting Austria. "I do not know," adds M. de Bausset, "whether to attribute the fact to her vexation at the circumspect Austrian diplomacy, or simply to her natural politeness and the sympathy she thought it her duty to feel for the innocent victim of a greater political convulsion than that of which she complained and which she had, in fact, provoked. In any case, it is certain that she had sufficient greatness of soul to appreciate the fidelity and devotion of those who had followed the fortunes of her granddaughter. Even in speaking of Napoleon, though she did so with the frankness of an enemy, yet it was that of an enemy not blind to his great qualities. Convinced by all the Empress said, that the Emperor had always treated her with the utmost kindness, and that she had been overwhelmed with the most touching and tender solicitude, the Queen of Sicily prevailed on her to wear again a portrait of Napoleon which her timidity had caused her to hide away in a jewel-case. Nor did she fail to be most amiable and caressing to the young Napoleon, though he was her enemy's son." M. de Bausset says very justly that such conduct displayed as much intelli gence as delicacy.

Marie Louise and her grandmother, Queen Marie Caroline, were together only a few weeks. The Empress went to Aix, in Savoy, June 29, 1814, to take the baths. They were never to meet again. On September 7 the old Queen went to bed, feeling very well. Two hours later she was found dead, with her right hand extended to the bell-rope she had been unable to reach, and her mouth half-open, as if she had vainly tried to call for assistance. A stroke of apoplexy had put a sudden term to her troubled career.

Baron de La Tour-du-Pin, then the French Minis- ter at Vienna, communicated the news to Prince Talleyrand in a despatch dated September 8, 1814: "I have the honor to inform you that the Queen of Naples had an attack of apoplexy during the night, which carried her off instantly. The Princess had never been in better health. That very morning Count de Préville, formerly an officer of the French navy, and now attached to that of the King of the Two Sicilies, had arrived here from Parma. He brought news from the King which fully satisfied the Queen. She approved the applications he had made to the Austrian court. The Queen kept M. de Préville with her all day, and chatted about Sicily and all her affairs with her usual vivacity. She sent him away at ten o'clock, and went to bed; at midnight, the maid who slept near her, hearing a slight movement, asked if she needed anything, and, receiving no answer, she rose, and found that the Queen was already dead."

She was buried at Vienna, with great pomp. Baron de La Tour-du-Pin wrote to Prince Talleyrand, September 14, 1814: "The obsequies of the Queen of Naples took place on the 10th; the Mass was celebrated on the 12th. The whole imperial family assisted at it, with the exception of the Empress. The Diplomatic Corps was not invited, as it is not customary. I thought, however, that the French Minister could hardly allow this circumstance to interfere with his giving some more particular mark of interest than was due from others, and I was present at the funeral. It seemed to me that they were pleased with this attention. Prince Leopold's sorrow has been most touching to everybody. On the day of his mother's death he sent a messenger to Madame the Duchess of Orleans [Marie Amélie, daughter of Marie Caroline and wife of Louis Philippe], by whom the news was doubtless carried more quickly than by the one I sent Your Highness."

Marie Louise heard of her grandmother's death with great pain. In spite of the short time they had spent together, her sorrow was deep and keen. With Marie Caroline disappeared one of the most singular figures of the century.

IV.

MARIE LOUISE left Schoenbrunn, June 29, 1814, to take the baths at Aix in Savoy. She had found it somewhat difficult to obtain her father's permission to undertake a journey which must have appeared strange. In 1814 Savoy still belonged to France, and the former Empress of the French was going to live simply as a private person in a town whose sovereign she had been only three months before. Napoleon felt strongly the singularity of this proceeding. General Bertrand wrote to M. de Méneval from Porto-Ferrajo, July 3, 1814: "If the Empress has waited at Vienna for an answer to her letter, the Emperor desires that she should not go to Aix; if she is already there, that she should not remain more than one season, and that she should return as soon as may be to Tuscany, where there are baths which have the same properties as those of Aix. They are nearer to us and to Parma, and the Empress could have her son there with her. When M. Corvisart recommended the waters of Aix, he was reasoning as if the Emperor and she were still

31

at Paris; besides, he knew nothing of these Tuscan baths, which have similar qualities. Her going to Aix displeases the Emperor all the more because there are probably no Austrian troops there now, and she may be exposed to insults from adventurers. Moreover, it will doubtless be disagreeable to the sovereigns of the country to have her so near. There would be no such inconveniences in Tuscany."

But Marie Louise had taken good care not to wait for her husband's permission to start. She was determined to go to Aix, whose waters she deemed indispensable to her health, and where she expected to meet the Duchess of Montebello, whom she then considered her dearest friend. She left her son at Schoenbrunn, in charge of the Countess of Montesquiou, and started in company with the Baron of Méneval and the Countess of Brignole. She travelled as the Countess of Colorno, which was the name of one of her chateaux in the Duchy of Parma. When she passed through Munich she found Prince Eugene de Beauharnais and his wife at the station, and went to supper with them and the Princess Royal of Würtemberg, destined soon to become the fourth wife of the Austrian Emperor.

On the 10th of July Marie Louise reached the inn of Sécheron, close to Geneva. There she was met by her brother-in-law, King Joseph, who lived in the Villa Prangins on the shore of the lake, and who gave her a hearty welcome. As she seemed to regret not having ordered saddle-horses to be provided for her while at Aix, Joseph offered one of his own which was suitable, and she rode no other during her journey.

She made an excursion to Chamouni and the environs of Geneva which lasted six days, and on July 17 arrived at Aix in Savoy. Just as she was about to enter the town she met a man on horseback and wearing the uniform of an Austrian general, who bowed profoundly and then turned to escort her. Doubtless, she would have been greatly surprised had any one then predicted to her the part this man was to play in her existence. He was forty-two — twenty years older than she. He had but one eye; a black bandage hid the deep scar of the wound which had deprived him of the other. At the first glance his aspect was anything rather than seductive. It was General Count Neipperg, who had acted as chamberlain to Marie Louise during her stay at Prague in 1812, shortly after the conference at Dresden. She had not noticed him then, and had never seen him since. The singular attachment she was to feel for him was by no means a case of love at first sight. The wily diplomatist had neither the beauty, the youth, nor the prestige which conquer without an effort. M. de Méneval declares that when she met him before Aix she found him uncongenial. "His appearance," says he, "gave her a disagreeable impression, which she did not try to hide. Was it the instinct of a heart honest but distrustful of itself which revealed him as her evil genius, and secretly warned her against yielding to his designs?"

At this time Marie Louise had not yet broken all
the ties which united her to her husband. She still
wrote to him. Her household was composed of
ardent Bonapartists like M. de Bausset and M. de
Méneval. She had left her son under the care of a
Frenchwoman, the Countess of Montesquiou, whose
admiration for the Emperor was profound. She had
invited a widow of a marshal of France, the Duchess
of Montebello, to stay with her. Her maid of honor
was the Countess of Brignole, a noble lady not less
devoted to Napoleon than the Countess of Montesquiou.

With the exception of General Neipperg, all those
who approached her during her stay at Aix, — Isabey,
who painted her portrait; Talma, who recited verses
to her; Baron Corvisart, who was her physician;
Baron de Bausset and Count de Cussy, who acted
by turns as chamberlain, — all were imperialists who
still cherished an actual veneration for Napoleon.
Her servants were French, both men and women.
Her coachmen and footmen still wore the imperial
livery, and the arms of France were painted on the
panels of her carriages and engraved upon her silver.
Nevertheless, the Bourbons must have believed her
very unlikely to aid seriously her husband's cause,
or her residence in a French watering-place would
not have troubled them so little.

And yet Marie Louise was on all sides surrounded
by souvenirs of the Empire. The house she lived in,
situated on a little hill above Aix, was that which

Queen Hortense had occupied. This pretty town, so picturesque and poetic in its situation and the beauty of its environs, has had the privilege of con-soling dispossessed sovereigns. Josephine, deprived of the crowns of France and Italy, and Hortense, de-prived of that of Holland, appointed a meeting there in 1810. When one goes there first, the sombre moun-tains which rise like the citadels of God, and tower above the clouds floating about their summits, awaken a sentiment which is almost awe. But one soon learns to love these mountains, whose air is so pure, so vivifying, and that beautiful Lake Bourget, which sparkles or pales according to the clouds and the time of day. Marie Louise loved to go boating on it, and to visit the abbey of Haute-Combe on its shore, where the princes of the house of Savoy are buried. Its sepulchral silence, interrupted only by the monoto-nous chant of white-robed monks, is well calculated to inspire Christian reflections on the nothingness and inanity of worldly grandeur.

Marie Louise was very sad during the early days of her stay at Aix. A real warfare had begun within her soul between her two countries, Austria and France ; she understood the false position she was in, and suffered in silence, for her perplexities were not un-mingled with remorse. Her love for Count Neipperg had not yet begun. His audiences with her were purely official, and she did not suspect that he would one day take the place beside her which belonged to the Emperor Napoleon. M. de Méneval had left her, July 19, to pay his wife a visit of several weeks; but she kept up a close correspondence with him, and her letters show both the tumult in her soul and the confidence she continued to repose in one of the most faithful of her husband's adherents.

"I shall never succeed in persuading myself to return to Vienna until the sovereigns have departed," she wrote to M. de Méneval, August 9, 1814; "and I will put off seeing my son until then. I shall remain at Geneva or in Parma until the Congress; for it is impossible for me to stay here after the season of the baths is ended. I beg you to assist my determination by your counsel. Do not fear to tell me the truth. I ask advice from you as from a friend, and I hope you will give it to me frankly. I have just received a letter from the Emperor, dated July 4. He begs me not to go to Aix, but to take some baths in Tuscany. I have written to my father about it. You know how much I desire to please the Emperor; but, in this case, ought I to do so if his wishes do not agree with the intentions of my father?"

Her letter terminated thus: "I send you a letter from Porto-Ferrajo. I was greatly tempted to open it; it might have given me some details. If there are any, I beg you to let me know. I thank you much for those you sent; I needed them; I have had none for so long. On the whole, I am in a very unhappy and critical condition; it is very essential for me to be prudent in my conduct. There are moments when everything seems so strangely un-settled that I think the best thing I could do would be to die. . . . My health is good enough. I am at my tenth bath. They would be beneficial if my mind were easy, but I cannot be contented until I have got out of this miserable state of uncertainty. I rejoice to think that you will soon be here to talk reasonably to me, and to quiet my poor head." In a postscript the Empress added: "My son is wonder-fully well, so they write me, and becomes every day more charming. The days are long until I can see the poor child again."

The 15th of August came around to renew all the sorrows of the dethroned sovereign. She must have had some tender memories of both her husband and her son on that day, for it was the feast of each. To quote Victor Hugo: —

> " All drifts and passes with the sea,
>   World-masters, kings that cradled be,
>   Bald front, fair locks of infancy,
>   Great and little Napoleon ;
>   All vanish and themselves efface,
>   Surge upon surge rolls back apace,
>   Forgetting all, the billows pass,
>   Leviathan like Alcyon."

Marie Louise also was going to forget ; but on this day she had not yet forgotten. What a difference between those two dates : August 15, 1813 — August 15, 1814 ! What changes in one year ! At this time last year, France, exulting over the victories of

Lutzen and Bautzen, was expecting a speedy and glorious peace. Regent of the great Empire, Marie Louise, seated on her throne in the Tuileries, the imperial mantle on her shoulders, her head encircled with the most brilliant of the crown diamonds, had received the high officials who came to offer their homage and good wishes. Afterwards, she had assisted at a Solemn High Mass and a *Te Deum* in the castle chapel. In the evening she had been received with cries of joy and enthusiastic acclamations when she made her appearance on the balcony of the Hall of the Marshals, to listen to the concert given on the terrace, and see the fireworks go up from the Place de la Concorde. What a difference on August 15, 1814! Instead of the great illuminated capital, an obscure little town; instead of a numerous crowd of courtiers, a handful of attendants; instead of the Palace of the Tuileries, a humble white house; instead of the title of Empress of the French and Queen of Italy, that of the Duchess of Colorno; instead of the regency of a vast empire, the possession, or, more truly, the hope of an Italian duchy; instead of the King of Rome for a son, a poor child, of whom it was hardly known whether he would even obtain the right to be called the Prince of Parma.

The former Empress may never have been ambitious, but such contrasts could not fail to cast over her a sombre and melancholy veil. For her the day was one of sadness, not of joy. She wrote on that date to M. de Méneval: "I have not yet received an answer from my father to the letter I spoke of in my last. This time of uncertainty appears to me very cruel and very long. I await his reply with much impatience, and I will let you know the moment it arrives. A sad presentiment warns me that it will contain nothing pleasant; but this is one of my gloomy days. How can I be gay on this feast day, when I am obliged to spend it so far from the two persons who are dearest to me? Pardon these sad reflections; but the friendship you have always shown me gives me courage to make them, providing you will tell me when I weary you. I beg you to believe in my sincere friendship. Your affectionate LOUISE."

In a postscript Marie Louise refers to her disappointment in the matter of Parma. Count Marescalchi, formerly the Italian Minister of Foreign Affairs, an honorable man and well known as a sympathizer with France, had at first been charged with organizing the administration of the duchy, but the Austrian Cabinet had revoked his appointment. "M. de Marescalchi," wrote Marie Louise, "is simply the Austrian Minister at my court now; my father has appointed M. de San Vitale my grand-chamberlain, and without consulting me. This pains and exasperates me. M. Magawly said at Parma that my father had summoned M. de San Vitale to Vienna in order to perform his functions near me, and that I would be expected to go there and remain during the entire Congress. What a dreary prospect! I have a mind to ask him if I may pass the winter in Florence, providing that I promise not to communicate with the Emperor except through the Grand Duke, but I feel almost sure he would refuse. What I am determined on is not to go to Vienna while the sovereigns are there. Advise me, I pray you; I assure you I am greatly to be pitied."

Throughout this entire day her mind continually reverted to M. de Méneval. In the evening she wrote again, to apprise him that she had just received a letter from Prince Metternich in which he enjoined her, in the name of the Emperor of Austria, not to go to Parma. In this epistle she deplores her fate as she had done in the preceding one: "The Duchess of Montebello will tell you many things I cannot write about. I am sad, but resigned. To-morrow will give me the most painful blow, for then I must bid her adieu. But I will not complain; I must accustom myself to all sorts of trouble. What consoles me is the thought that there are still some kind souls who pity me, and I remember with pleasure that you are among the number."

Marie Louise no longer found it agreeable to remain at Aix when the Duchess of Montebello had departed. There was, in fact, no reason why she should prolong her stay, since her health was re-established. Moreover, although her conduct had been scrupulously prudent, yet the government of Louis XVIII. was beginning to be uneasy about her presence in a French town. Prince Talleyrand had written, August 9, 1814, to Prince Metternich: "When you were in Paris last, my dear Prince, you told the King you did not approve of the journey which Madame the Archduchess Marie Louise had made to the baths of Aix. From the moment that the waters became useful to her health, the King would have closed his eyes to the inconveniences of this journey if he saw any. But you, my dear Prince, thought it might give occasion, not to intrigues, but to a good deal of gossip. You know what the tattle of a watering-place amounts to, and what mischief these idle babblers may bring about. A few rattle-pates go far enough to compromise themselves, and it is just this which it is necessary to avoid. Joseph Bonaparte, who is near Aix, has committed follies which he would not have dreamed of but for her being there. All this is of very small importance, and the King attaches none to it; but rumors of it have reached Paris, and give occasion for random talk, to the Diplomatic Corps as well as to everybody else. People fancy they discover grave and secret intrigues at the bottom of things which are perfectly natural and simple. I fancy, my dear Prince, that since the season of the baths is over for Madame the Archduchess, it may suit both you and us if her stay at Aix should not be further prolonged. Do not misunderstand, however, the motives which induce me to make this suggestion. Adieu, my dear Prince; preserve a kindly regard for me, and believe in my sincere attachment for yourself."

Marie Louise might have wished to remain longer at Aix, but she would not have been permitted to do so. However, she still thought about her husband. August 20, she wrote to the Baron of Méneval: "I have news from the Emperor dated August 6. He is in good health, happy and tranquil, and thinks much about me and his son." But the time was approaching when the influence of Count Neipperg, who was gradually insinuating himself into her good graces, should detach her forever from Napoleon. She left Aix early in September, and before returning to Vienna she made an excursion into Switzerland, where Count Neipperg acted as her guide.

As to the sovereign of Elba, he already had forebodings that he would never again see either wife or son. A few weeks earlier he had still hoped for a reunion, which he desired above all things. He wrote to Count Bertrand from Porto-Ferrajo, July 27, 1814: "I have decided to go to Marciana on August 1. My house must be built during my absence, so that when the Empress comes it shall be ready for her." By August 9 his hopes had begun to weaken. Doubt is to be read between the lines of the letter he wrote that day to his Grand Marshal of the Palace: "M. le Comte de Bertrand, Colonel Laczinski, who starts to-day at two o'clock for Livorno, will go from there to Aix, bearing a letter from me to the Empress. Write to Méneval that I expect the Empress by the end of August; that I want her to fetch my son, and think it strange to receive no word from her, doubtless because her letters have been intercepted. This absurd performance is probably the work of some petty official; it cannot be that of her father. In any case, no one has any rights over the Empress and her son."

The people of Elba, however, believed firmly in the speedy arrival of the Empress and the King of Rome. Chateaubriand remarks in his *Mémoires d'outre-tombe:* "Every one expected to see Marie Louise and her son very soon. In reality, a woman with a child did appear. Great mystery surrounded her reception, and she went to stay in a lonely cottage in the remotest part of the island. On the shore of Ogygie Calypso told her love to Ulysses, who, instead of listening, thought only of defending himself against her advances. After two days of repose the swan of the north took her flight again toward the myrtles of Baiæ." This mysterious woman was the Countess Walewska, the beautiful Pole who had inspired the Emperor with such a passionate admiration some years before. Her son, born March 4, 1810, was nearly the same age as the King of Rome.

An eye-witness thus relates this singular incident of Napoleon's residence at Elba: "On the 1st of September, 1814, the Emperor spent the entire day on the heights of Pomonté, sweeping the sea with a small telescope, as if to discover and recognize all vessels which came in sight. At nightfall he re-entered the Hermitage and sent an orderly on horseback to Porto-

Ferrajo to provide a carriage and three saddle-horses, which were to wait the instructions of the Grand Marshal of the Palace, in the road leading to the Place Saint-Jean. At about ten in the evening the orderly was at the point indicated with the carriage and the horses. It was a fine moonlight night and he presently saw a rowboat approaching the jetty. Three ladies and a child landed from it, and General Bertrand, saluting them respectfully, led the way to the carriage. At the cross-roads of Prochia they met Napoleon riding a white horse and followed by a troop of lancers and Mamelukes. The carriage stopped, and the Emperor got off his horse. The right-hand door of the carriage opened, and the Emperor entered it in profound silence. The procession set off again and did not stop until it reached the beach of Prochia, where, as the carriage could go no farther on account of the bad roads, the Emperor, the ladies, and the child left it for the horses, which had been led by the orderly. The child was carried by one of the ladies, and the orderly, dismounting, led her horse by the bridle. When they were near the Hermitage, Napoleon spurred up his horse and arrived first at a tent which had been pitched under a huge chestnut. A few minutes later the lady with the child came up and entered the tent also. They remained there two days and nights without being seen by any one else. Napoleon himself came out only twice to give some orders. During this time all persons were forbidden access to the hill, even Madame Mère, who lodged in a neighboring village."

Thus, at the very moment when Marie Louise was beginning to yield to Count Neipperg's influence, Napoleon, despairing of seeing her at Elba, had bethought himself of the Countess Walewska.

V.

MARIE LOUISE IN SWITZERLAND.

THE last sparks of a very feeble flame are about to be extinguished. In Switzerland the former Empress of the French is already less attached to Napoleon than she had been at Aix in Savoy. The hour is near when he will be as a stranger to her. The influence of MM. de Méneval and de Bausset diminishes as that of Count Neipperg increases. Marie Louise, to whom the thought of being in Vienna at the same time with the sovereigns was once so painful, is now accustoming herself to entertain it. Count Neipperg never leaves her. If she boldly undertakes so many fatiguing, not to say dangerous, excursions across mountains and glaciers, it is because the seducer is at her side. He is a musician, and when she sings, he plays her accompaniments. He is an assiduous, devoted, obsequious chamberlain; perhaps he is already a lover. He will presently become her factotum, her indispensable attendant. He vaunts his ability to solve all difficulties and smooth away all obstacles which lie between her and that Duchy of Parma which she thinks of as a Promised Land.

Agent and confidant of Prince Metternich, he pursues with address and perseverance the task confided to him by the Austrian oligarchy. He is neither young nor handsome, but there is something alluring in his glance, his appearance, and his conversation. His uniform as general of hussars becomes him; his manners are extremely polished, and they hide his ardent ambition under a cloak of modest simplicity. A brave soldier and a skilful diplomatist, he has the good taste never to talk about himself, although he both talks and writes with ease. Marie Louise no longer even thinks of rejoining her husband at Elba. Perhaps she would not do so even if her father accorded his permission. Her sole ambition is to reign in Parma, with the faithful Neipperg as her minister. She has forgotten France. It seems as if she had said an eternal adieu to the country where she had reigned, when parting from the Duchess of Montebello, the only Frenchwoman whom she had loved.

Marie Louise appreciated the beauties of nature, and she greatly enjoyed herself in Switzerland; possibly the proximity of Count Neipperg, who acted as guide, helped to make her find that land so charming. September 9, 1814, she slept at Lausanne, at Freiburg the 10th, and at Berne on the 11th. Then she visited Grinwal, Lauterburn, and the Righi, with the Countess of Brignole and General Neipperg for sole attendants. "M. de Méneval and I," writes the Baron of Bausset, "had seen snow enough in Russia. We were not particularly anxious to wander among those mountains all covered with it." So these two left the field to the General, who, doubtless, was not sorry.

September 20, Marie Louise came back to Berne. She had just heard of the death of her grandmother, Queen Marie Caroline, and she displayed great sorrow. For two days she shut herself up in her apartments, but on September 22 she made an excursion to Hofhill, two leagues from Berne. On returning, she was informed of the arrival of the Princess of Wales, whom she did not know, but who desired to meet her. This Princess was, assuredly, one of the most curious types of our modern times. Her father was Charles William Ferdinand, Duke of Brunswick, a bitter enemy of the French Revolution, the author of the celebrated manifesto of 1792, and the unsuccessful opponent of Dumouriez and Napoleon. Caroline was born in 1768, and in 1795 was married to the Prince of Wales. In the following year she became the mother of the Princess Charlotte, who was afterwards the wife of Leopold, King of Belgium. Hardly had she recovered from her confinement when her husband separated from her on the plea of incompatibility of temper. Then began recriminations and scandals which resounded throughout Europe, and never ceased until the death of Caroline.

Her husband, the Prince of Wales, whose whole youth had been turbulent, and who had many things to reproach himself with, noisily accused his wife of adultery; claiming, even, that she had concealed a pregnancy. In 1808, her father-in-law, George III., appointed a ministerial commission to examine these charges. They acquitted her, so far as the latter accusation was concerned, declaring, at the same time, that her conduct had been imprudent. When George III. went mad, in 1811, the Prince of Wales became Regent. It was of him that Louis XVIII. said: "After God, it is to the Prince-Regent that I owe my restoration."

Caroline, then, was daughter of one man, and wife of another, of those who were most bitterly hostile to Napoleon. Nevertheless, she was anxious to see Marie Louise, and even proposed to pay a visit to Napoleon himself, at Elba. When she met the former Empress of the French at Berne, she was beginning a long journey. After passing through Germany, she meant to visit Italy, Greece, Syria, and the Holy Land. Caroline was witty and agreeable, and she spoke French admirably. All was unusual about her, — face, figure, dress, and conversation. She wore a white muslin gown, and a large veil of the same stuff, which covered her head, breast, and shoulders. Above this was a diadem consisting of a single row of diamonds. Her costume resembled that of an ancient Greek priestess.

In the morning of September 23 this noble but eccentric traveller had her first interview with Marie Louise, to whom she showed herself extremely friendly. She gave her all manner of details concerning her quarrel with her husband, and the annoyances to which she had recently been subjected in England. "Your Majesty will hardly believe," said she, "that I was not permitted to attend the Queen's drawing-room while the sovereigns of Russia and Prussia were there, because my husband was unwilling to meet me, either in public or in private. I complained to the Queen, and I even wrote my husband a beautiful letter, in which I signed myself the most faithful and submissive of wives [the Princess smiled maliciously while saying these last words]; but he did not deign to answer me. However, I did not consider myself obliged to observe strict seclusion on that account. I went to every public place to which I could gain admittance by paying my way. Once, when the sovereigns and my husband were at the opera, in a box in the dress-circle, I was discovered at the back of another, on the second tier, where I had gone in disguise. The people showed their good will toward me by such stormy applause, that these august spectators, supposing it impossible that so much homage could be addressed to any one but themselves, thought it incumbent on them to rise and bow to the audience. I was not slow in seizing this chance to avenge myself. Pretending, in my turn, to consider their mistake as an intentional act of politeness toward me, I gravely made them three sweeping courtesies, which excited loud and ironical applause."

Caroline spoke afterwards of her daughter, the

Princess Charlotte. "She is as charming and clever as one can possibly be; but," she added, smiling, "after myself, I don't know a more quarrelsome person."

In the evening the Princess of Wales, accompanied by a lady-of-honor, two chamberlains, and an equerry, came to dine with Marie Louise, who had returned her visit during the day. The dinner was very lively, and afterwards, the conversation turning on music, the Empress invited the Princess to sing something. "Willingly," she replied, "providing that it shall be a duet." Marie Louise wished to refuse, under the plea of her timidity, which, she said, made her incapable of uttering a note before listeners. "For my part," responded the Princess of Wales, "I have never been afraid, except on account of my friends." Marie Louise finally consented. Her voice was a soprano, as sweet and pleasing as herself; Caroline's, on the contrary, was a full and strongly accented contralto, which accorded well with her energetic character. They sang the duet *La ci darem la mano*, from Mozart's *Don Juan*, Count Neipperg playing the accompaniment, Marie Louise taking the part of Zerlina, and Caroline that of Don Juan. Would not the scene be a tempting one for a *genre* painter?

September 24, the Empress slept at Zurich. She visited some glaciers in the neighborhood, as well as the ruined castle of Hapsburg, the cradle of her ancestors. Some one of the party found an old scrap of iron among the ruins, and Count Neipperg pretended to recognize in it a fragment of Rudolph of Hapsburg's lance. Marie Louise either believed, or professed to believe, in this little fraud, and, later on, had bits of the chimerical lance set in gold rings, which she gave to various members of her circle.

She went on to Vienna by way of Saint-Gall, Constance, Munich, and Braunau, and passed the night in the latter city. It was the place where, on March 16, 1810, the house of Austria had formally committed her to the house of France. That day of profound emotions lay already far behind her. The Empire, that majestic and colossal edifice, which all men had thought indestructible, had disappeared. It had lasted not much longer than the frail walls of the pavilion where the young Archduchess had been confided to her new country. At that time the same ceremonies had been observed as had attended the marriage of Marie Antoinette. Triumphal arches had spanned the roads traversed by the august betrothed. To the sound of bells, the roar of artillery, and the joyous flourish of trumpets, she had appeared before the dazzled eyes of the people like a sort of goddess, illuminated by the lustres of an apotheosis. And now, at the end of four years and a half, she was again at Braunau, alas, under what different conditions! She was travelling as a private person, bearing the assumed title of Duchess of Colorno. Nothing but the memory of those distant splendors was left to her, and it is doubtful if even that memory was dear. Soon it was to vanish like a dream. Marie Louise returned to Schoenbrunn, October 4, 1814, the feast of Saint Francis of Assisi, and the name-day of her father. From that moment nothing that was French remained longer in her Austrian soul.

VI.

"WHO would believe that the lust after pageants, the bursts of applause which greet Molière and Harlequin at the theatres, the hunts and banquets, ballets and tournaments, cover so many disquieting cares and opposing interests, such fears and hopes, such ardent passions, and such serious affairs?"

One is reminded of this passage from La Bruyère when studying the history of that Vienna Congress, of which the Prince de Ligne said: "The Congress dances; it does not walk." The sovereigns made their formal entry into the Austrian capital September 26, 1814. More than a thousand volleys of cannon greeted them from the ramparts. A contemporary caricature represents the Emperor Alexander driving a two-seated travelling-carriage, with the King of Prussia as footman, and the Emperor Napoleon running behind, and shouting to the Emperor Francis, "Father-in-law! father-in-law! they have put me out." The Austrian Emperor, who occupies the carriage, looks back, and answers, "And me in."

The presence of Marie Louise in a city where the

sovereigns who had vanquished and dethroned her
husband were reunited was singular enough. Five
days after her return to the castle of Schoenbrunn,
a fête was given there which all the monarchs attended. There were drives about the gardens in
open carriages, theatricals, and a supper in the
Orangery. But the former Empress of the French
remained in the seclusion of her own apartments.
On November 9, 1814, Baron de La Tour-du-Pin,
French Minister at Vienna, wrote as follows to
Count de Jaucourt, who acted as Minister of Foreign Affairs during the absence of Prince Talleyrand: "The Archduchess Marie Louise is never
present at any of the fêtes and daily reunions which
are brought about by circumstances. But she comes
every day to see her father, and often calls on the
sovereigns and grand duchesses who are staying at
the palace. She is visited in return at Schoenbrunn,
but not so as to attract too much attention. Her
toilet seems to occupy her greatly, and no week
passes without her receiving gowns and bonnets from
Paris. At the same time, melancholy speeches escape her lips; she plays doleful airs, and says that
she was made for sadness. They take pains to let
it be known that the little Bonaparte has remarkable intelligence, and he is so trained as to make him
pleasing to the French, and especially to soldiers.
It appears that whenever one presents himself, or
when he speaks of them, he is expected to say
gracious and kindly things. The fêtes increase in-

stead of diminishing. Yesterday M. de Metternich gave one; day after to-morrow there will be a grand dress rout, and on the 16th a tournament composed of twenty-four ladies and as many cavaliers."

One might say that Marie Louise could only look through the keyhole at these entertainments where her presence was forbidden. In her father's apartments at the Burg, the imperial palace of Vienna, a small tribune or platform had been so placed in a corner of the upper gallery surrounding the great hall that one could see from it without being seen. It was the same great hall in which the festivities of her marriage had taken place in 1810. Hidden at the back of this tribune with M. de Bausset and Madame de Brignole, what reflections the dethroned sovereign must have made! She had seen at her own knees the same crowd of noble lords and ladies who now paid such assiduous court to the princes of the Coalition. How humble and obsequious all these petty potentates of the Rhine Confederation had been but lately before the great Napoleon! His wife might have said, with the author of the *Dieu des bonnes gens:* —

> " A conq'ror in his lofty hour of pride
>   With laws and sceptres played as trifling things;
>   The dust from off his feet men saw
>   Imprinted on the coronets of Kings.
>   You crawled then, Kings, whom now men deify!"

Who was the princess now disputing so bitterly the possession of the duchies of Parma, Piacenza, and Guastalla with Marie Louise? It was she who had been created Queen of Etruria by a caprice of the First Consul. Tuscany was erected into the Kingdom of Etruria by the Treaty of Lunéville, and given to Louis, Infant of Parma; and in May, 1801, before taking possession of his states, he went to receive investiture, as it were, from Bonaparte. He was the son of a sister of Marie Antoinette, and his wife, who accompanied him, was the daughter of Charles IV. of Spain. It was only seven years since Marie Antoinette had lost her head on the scaffold, and her nephew in going to Malmaison to pay homage to the First Consul crossed the square where she was executed. At the Théâtre Français they played *Œdipe* in his honor, and when the actor who took the part of Philoctète recited the verse,

" I have made sovereigns, and I have not willed to be one,"

the audience turned toward the box where the First Consul was sitting with his royal guest, and broke into a frenzy of applause which shook the theatre. Oh! how insignificant this kinglet had seemed beside the man of Arcole, the Pyramids, and Marengo! A few days later the new King and Queen departed for Etruria, where they were installed by Murat. The Queen presently opened a friendly and grateful correspondence with Josephine, by whose gracious reception of herself and her husband she had been charmed. Assuredly, the all-powerful First Consul would have been profoundly surprised had any seer then come to tell him: "It is this little Queen who will one day seek to deprive your wife and son of the only strip of land remaining to them after all your conquests!"

Marie Louise was present at the general rehearsal of the tournament, which took place in the Hall of the Manège. This hall is a long parallelogram, terminating at each end in a large tribune. One of these was occupied by the sovereigns, and the other by the orchestra. Opposite the monarchs, in a tier of boxes placed in front of the musicians, were sedately ranged the twenty-four ladies of the twenty-four knights about to combat in the lists. All of them beautiful and full of animation, they were clad in red velvet robes against which the lustre of their jewels sparkled with great effect. The gems worn by Princess Paul Esterhazy, born Princess de la Tour et Taxis, were valued at more than six millions of francs. The fête was magnificent. The twenty-four knights, in splendid costumes, and mounted on superb and richly caparisoned palfreys, entered to the flourish of trumpets. Riding forward, they made their reverence to the sovereigns without dismounting; then, turning, they paid a similar homage to the ladies whose colors and scarfs they wore. They tilted at the ring, beat down helmets which had been placed upon manikins, and handled harmless javelins with precision. The tourney ended, each cavalier rejoined his lady and conducted her to the banqueting-hall. From the feast they repaired to the ball-room, where more than three thousand invited guests were present. The quadrilles, which had been arranged beforehand, were comprised of the most illustrious and highly born men and women in all Germany. Concerning the second representation of the tournament, Baron de La Tour-du-Pin wrote on November 30, 1814, to Count de Jaucourt: "This fête has been perfectly beautiful, and the splendor of the women has exceeded anything ever seen. One might more truly say that they were clothed with diamonds and precious stones than that they were adorned with them. The ladies had given scarfs to their knights; that presented by Madame de Perigord to Count de Trautmansdorff, the Grand-Equerry, was sown with golden flowers-de-luce, with lion's claws in the fringe. We were childish enough to feel pleased because this knight carried off the honors of the day."

Meanwhile, serious people were beginning to think there was a good deal of amusement going on at Vienna. Seldom have important affairs been treated with so much apparent levity. Prince de Talleyrand wrote to Louis XVIII., on November 25, 1814: "After I left Prince de Metternich, he went to the Ridotto, for he spends three-quarters of his time at balls and public entertainments. His head was so full of the Naples business that, having met there a woman of his acquaintance, he told her that he was being tormented about it, but that he did not know how to give his consent. He said he respected a man who had made himself beloved in the country he governed; and that, moreover, he loved the Queen passionately, and was in constant relations with her. All this, and perhaps a little more on the same head, was said under the mask." In his new capacity as courtier of Louis XVIII. Talleyrand could not pardon Metternich for preserving his affection for Napoleon's sister, and wishing to protect in Murat a prince whom the Bourbons considered an upstart and usurper.

The Austrian Minister was also the object of some sharp criticism at the hands of Baron de La Tour-du-Pin, who wrote to Count de Jaucourt, December 7, 1814: "The public generally are discontented with the condition of affairs; they especially find fault with the Emperor of Russia, who loses in public estimation daily. Any minister but M. de Metternich would take immense advantage of this; but what can be expected of a man who, in the gravest situation that can possibly be imagined, spends the greater portion of his time in follies; who was not afraid to have the *Pacha de Surène* played at his house, and who, ever since the Congress began, has spent a good many of his days in an equally futile way? After this, M. le Conte, you ought not to be surprised at the slow progress of affairs."

This *Pacha de Surène*, which was one of the Baron de La Tour-du-Pin's grievances, had the greatest success at one of the court soirées. Étienne's charming comedy was played in French by amateurs, who were the Landgrave of Furstenburg, Prince Antoine Radzi-

will, Count Ferdinand de Waldstein, Countess Mnis-
check, Princess Theresa Esterhazy, Princess Marie de
Metternich, Countess Marassi, Princesses Marie and
Sophie de Lichtenstein, etc. After the play followed
tableaux in which some of the most distinguished
persons of the court took part. The principal one
was the Tent of Darius, after Lebrun's painting.
Count de Schoenfeld represented Alexander the
Great, and the beautiful Countess Sophie Zichy,
Statira. Baron de Bausset writes enthusiastically in
his Memoirs: " The scene was at once heroic and
voluptuous; all the faces, all the attitudes of the
figures in this living picture, wore expressions suitable to their age, their condition, and their situation.
Sizygambis herself was admirable."

On December 2, 1814, a grand rout was held at
the imperial palace, of which an account is found in
a letter from Vienna published in the *Moniteur
Universel*. Three great halls were thrown into one
by means of galleries and staircases, thus providing
a space so large that ten or twelve thousand people
might easily move round in it. The passage conducting from the apartments of the palace to this
grand hall was adorned with shrubbery and flowers,
and looked like fairy-land. An alley lined with
orange-trees led to the great hall, whence could be
seen, beyond a double staircase, the superb perspec-
tive afforded by the grounds of the riding-school.
The hall was decorated in white and silver, and
sparkled with five or six thousand candles. At ten

o'clock the sovereigns entered, to the blare of the trumpets and kettle-drums. The Czar and the Empress of Russia opened the march, followed by the Emperor and Empress of Austria, the King of Denmark and the Archduchess Beatrix, the King of Bavaria and the Grand Duchess of Oldenburg. Having passed several times through the three halls, the sovereigns seated themselves on a platform in the Hall of the Manège, and watched a ballet danced by masked children. The fête lasted until morning.

On that same day, December 2, the double anniversary of Napoleon's coronation and the battle of Austerlitz, Marie Louise had paid a visit to the Russian Empress, who was at the Burg. While the former Empress of the French was with the Czarina, her carriage was awaiting her upon the ramparts near by. Some of the curious bystanders who flocked about it observed that the carriage panels, the escutcheons of the harness, and the buttons on the livery of the footmen still bore the imperial arms of France. This offended them, and when Marie Louise re-entered her carriage they made remarks on the subject which she could not fail to hear. Nothing more was needed to induce her to have these arms removed. She replaced them by her own monogram.

Alas! it was not merely the imperial arms which the forgetful wife effaced; it was the memory of her husband. The captive of the Coalition, she began to familiarize herself with her chains and to love

Count Neipperg. Ever since her visit to Aix and Switzerland she had placed confidence in this man who was as much her guardian as her chamberlain. Baron de la Tour-du-Pin had written to Count de Jaucourt, on September 7, 1814: "I do not know whether you have been informed that Major-General the Count of Neipperg has been appointed by the Austrian Emperor as the guardian of his daughter. His business is to prevent her doing anything which might annoy or even displease the King; and, especially, to watch her carefully in case she seems disposed to go to her husband. Should that happen, he is to advise her against doing so, and, if she persists, to forbid it absolutely."

General Neipperg had acquitted himself of his mission to the entire satisfaction of his government. Marie Louise, who had once declared that nothing could induce her to go near the sovereigns who dethroned her, had ended by resigning herself with a good grace, not only to live in their neighborhood, but to receive their visits. Enchanted with the wily Neipperg's success, the Emperor of Austria desired him to act as her chamberlain throughout the Congress. He assumed, in fact, the duties of grand equerry and official chargé d'affaires as well as those of chamberlain. And in proportion as his influence over the weak young woman's mind increased, she repelled still further all thought of a reunion with Napoleon. A widow during the lifetime of her husband, she ceased to correspond with him. At first

he protested against this silence, which he did not
fully comprehend.   On October 10, 1814, he wrote
thus to an uncle of Marie Louise, Ferdinand Joseph,
Grand Duke of Tuscany, that Prince who had been
so respectful toward the Napoleonic glories, and so
assiduous at the court of the Tuileries when, as
Grand Duke of Wurzburg, he was a member of the
Rhine Confederation under the protectorate of the
new Charlemagne : —

"MY BROTHER AND VERY DEAR UNCLE: Hav·
ing received no news from my wife since August 10,
nor from my son for six months, I charge the Cheva-
lier Colonna with this letter.   I beg Your Royal
Highness to let me know whether I may send you a
letter for the Empress every week, and if you will
forward me her replies and those of the Countess of
Montesquiou, my son's governess.   I flatter myself
that, in spite of the events which have changed so
many persons, Your Royal Highness still preserves
some friendship for me."

The Grand Duke despatched this letter to Vienna.
Let us hear what M. de Méneval has to tell us about
the way it was received.   " One day," he says, " on
returning from her daily visit to the imperial palace,
Marie Louise brought back a letter from the Emperor
Napoleon which her father had given her.   The
Emperor complained of her silence, and begged her
to write him accounts of herself and her son.   The
letter had been delivered by a courier of the Grand
Duke of Tuscany, and the Austrian Emperor had

had it in his hands four days. It had been shown to the sovereigns without any doubt, for it was with that intention, and in order to prove his good faith to the Allies, that the Emperor Francis required his daughter to pass over to him all letters received from her husband. The Empress did not reply to this epistle, as she received no permission to do so."

At the instance of Prince Metternich, Marie Louise had promised not to hold any communication with her husband without the consent of her father, to whom she also remitted all letters which reached her from Elba. Napoleon, on learning that even his private letters to his wife were not respected, and that she was forbidden to reply, ceased writing to her altogether.

Yet a feeble tie still bound Marie Louise to her souvenirs of France. The Countess of Brignole, the Baron of Bausset, and the Baron of Méneval were still with her, and the Countess of Montesquiou continued to be the governess of the child who had been the King of Rome. M. de Méneval says : "The first day of 1815 reanimated in the heart of the Empress those memories of France which had been so violently assailed. It is kept as a holy-day in France, but in Vienna no one observes it. It is during the preceding week that people make presents and pay compliments. The streets of Vienna are crowded with carriages and pedestrians in their Sunday clothes. They seem to be burying the old year with honor rather than celebrating the birth of a new one. For a moment the Empress's return to French ways made us believe that all was not yet forgotten at Schoenbrunn. After Mass she received all her household in the gallery of the palace. She was so amiable as to offer me some charming gifts, products of Viennese industry, and to add to them one of those little picture-cards, expressive of good will, which it is a German custom to give one's friends at certain seasons of the year. Even Count Neipperg was cordial and attentive."

On January 6, Feast of the Three Kings, Marie Louise gave a luncheon to her son, her sisters, and her youngest brother, the little Archduke Francis, father of the present Emperor. The King of Rome found the bean in his slice of Twelfth Night cake, and enjoyed the ephemeral royalty it gives — a symbol of that which destiny had torn from him. Alas, the little Bonaparte, as he was now called by those who had strewn flowers and burned incense before his cradle, already had enemies! This child, not yet four years old, inspired the Coalition with fear. The least marks of good will shown toward him alarmed the zealous adherents of Louis XVIII. On August 13, 1814, Baron de la Tour-du-Pin had written to Talleyrand: " At present the little Bonaparte is alone at Schoenbrunn. It is certain that the Emperor of Austria shows him much affection. He receives the honors of an archduke." On October 15 M. de Talleyrand, somewhat reassured, wrote to the King: "Bonaparte's son is no longer treated as he was on his first arrival at Vienna. They dress him more simply, and have replaced his broad ribbon of the Legion of Honor by that of Saint Stephen."

M. de Méneval says that no real kindness was shown to Marie Louise and her son except by her father and her sisters. Her step-mother and her brothers-in-law talked of nothing but making the child a bishop. The Emperor was sometimes obliged to silence them. Baron de Bausset also mentions these hostile dispositions. He says: "It was the general opinion in Vienna that Napoleon ought to be sent to Saint Helena, because Elba was too close to Italy and France. As to his son, he should be educated for the priesthood, and made to hide under a wretched frock that heritage of glory and grandeur whose very memory they wished to extinguish."

The son of the great Emperor was already lovable and attractive. To his infant graces there was added a nameless and precocious melancholy. As the poet Coppée has so well said, he was

"A young eaglet, vaguely feeling himself a prisoner,"

and he inspired a tender sympathy in every generous soul. Listen to the faithful Méneval, who speaks of him with such touching and unreserved devotion: "My greatest distraction was to spend a few hours in the apartment of the young Prince. His pretty ways, his gentleness, and the vivacity of his repartees were charming; he was then nearly four years old. His fresh and rosy face was lighted by beautiful blue eyes and framed in clustering fair curls. His intelligence was precocious; he was better instructed, moreover, than many older children. Madame de Montesquiou never left him, even at night, and cared for him with all the solicitude of a mother. They rose at seven every morning, and, as soon as prayers were over, his daily lessons began. He not only read fluently, but even knew a little history and geography. One Abbé Lanti, almoner of the French Legation, came to talk Italian with him, and a valet de chambre addressed him only in German. The child could already make himself understood in both languages, but he disliked extremely to speak the latter, finding the pronunciation difficult and harsh." Already the heart of the former King of Rome, now the Prince of Parma, and awaiting the day when he should be merely the Duke of Reichstadt, was conscious of a strife between France, his true fatherland, and Austria, the false one they were imposing on him! Ah! what would not Napoleon have given to see his son, if only for one instant! Marie Louise, more fortunate, could behold him. But there must have been moments when the sight of this child, whose father she had abandoned, became a mute reproach.

There was at Vienna, at the time of the Congress, an amiable and celebrated old man who was the courtier of Marie Louise as he had been of Marie Antoinette, and who took a lively interest in the great Emperor's son. This octogenarian was Prince de Ligne, whose life had been so brilliant and who still wore with elegance his field-marshal's uniform. He was present at all the entertainments, and, wishing still to play his old rôle of arbiter of manners and good taste, he was naïvely astonished that he produced less effect on women than he had done fifty or sixty years before. " My time is over, my world is dead," he would say with gentle melancholy. " But after all, what merit is there in youth that people should lavish such favors on it? . . . It is disgusting to see what a brigandage of success it has in society."

The old man consoled himself by playing soldiers with the little Napoleon. It was he who said, " Honors, ribbons, glory itself, do they give as much pleasure as the first doll, the first sailor-suit? The child eats four times a day; the hero often cannot even take his supper." The first time he saw the little Prince he was thus announced: " Monseigneur, here is the Marshal Prince de Ligne." " Is he a marshal?" asked the child. " Yes, Monseigneur." " Is he one of those who deserted my father?"

One day when he had been much impressed by the military parade at the funeral of General Delmotte, the child gave his old friend an enthusiastic account of the pleasure he felt at the sight of so many fine troops. " I will give you a greater satisfaction than that before long," answered Prince de Ligne; " the funeral of a field-marshal is the most magnificent thing of the sort that can be." The old man kept his word. He died during the Congress, and, between two balls, procured the sight of a splendid funeral for the sovereigns. Ten thousand troops under arms escorted his coffin to the Kahlenberg, the last mountain of the immense Alpine chain. There he was buried in a pavilion he had dedicated to Gaiety and the Muses, not far from the chapel where John Sobieski went to pray on the day when he delivered Vienna. The Prince de Ligne died a Christian. It was he who said apropos of some blatant professions of infidelity: " All this is very fine when one does not hear the bell for the dying. Really, unbelief is so much a pretence, that if a man honestly had it, I don't see why he shouldn't kill himself at the first pain of mind or body. No one understands sufficiently what human nature would be under the influence of positive irreligion. As to the atheists, they are living under the protection of religion."

In the midst of entertainments of all sorts there was even found a place for preachers. The fashionable sermons were those of the famous tragic poet, Werner, once a Lutheran, but now converted to Catholicity and in holy orders. The King of Prussia said to him one day, " I don't like people who change their religion." " That's why I don't like Luther," he responded. The Abbé Werner was a success, both as preacher and as poet. His sermons and his verses gave equal pleasure. Marie Louise invited him to Schoenbrunn, and he read her his tragedy, *Cunégonde.*

But as to the gayer entertainments, they went on without Marie Louise sharing in them. For one day, January 21, 1815, they were interrupted by a mass of expiation, offered as homage to the memory of the martyr-king. The sovereigns, all in mourning, repaired to the Cathedral of Saint Stephen for this solemnity. Who was the man who took the initiative in the matter? It was the former bishop who had said mass in the Champ de Mars on the day of the Fête of the Federation; the minister of the Directory who, on the 18th Fructidor, was the implacable enemy of the Royalists; the grand chamberlain of Napoleon who, on the day of his coronation, carried the casket intended to receive the Emperor's mantle.

The memory of the execution of Louis XVI. did not afflict the sovereigns very long. The next day after this doleful anniversary there was a splendid fête at Schoenbrunn. The monarchs and princes came out from Vienna in sleighs which they drove themselves. Superb horses drew them, decked with splendid plumes and shaking silver bells. A large detachment of cavalry opened the march. One immense sleigh was filled with trumpeters and drummers who made a prodigious noise. All the ladies were wrapped in magnificent furs. The procession drove through the courts and gardens of Schoenbrunn; afterwards they entered the palace, and even passed through the apartments of Madame de Montesquiou and Madame de Brignole. They respected those only of Marie Louise, who, hidden in her chamber, listened to the blaring of the trumpets. After a sumptuous banquet everybody repaired to the theatre of the castle, where a German version of *Cinderella* was represented. This sleigh-ride cost between five and six hundred thousand francs.

It was a singular idea to place Marie Louise in the midst of this whirlpool of pleasure in which she was forbidden to take part. The joyous music which resounded for others, but not for her, must have brought ironic echoes to her ears. "To me also," she might have said, "fêtes have been given. I, too, have been the object of public curiosity and universal enjoyment. I, too, have been flattered by courtiers never tired of telling me I possessed all graces and all virtues."

The former Empress of the French, who was even now but twenty-three, had already recovered from many illusions and human vanities. Nevertheless she still had one ambition: it was to be the Duchess of Parma. Her whole mind was bent on this, and General Neipperg was careful to cherish her fixed idea. He harped upon it continually, and with a zeal which made her believe him the only man really interested in her fate. In spite of the formal stipulations of the treaty of Fontainebleau, made on April 11, 1814, the Spanish and French plenipotentiaries wished to deprive her of the duchies of Parma, Piacenza, and Guastalla, and give them to the former Queen of Etruria, the daughter of Charles IV.

of Spain. Prince Talleyrand, contrary to all equity and justice, combated bitterly the indisputable rights of Napoleon's wife. On January 19, 1815, he wrote to Louis XVIII.: " As to the arrangements now making with reference to Italian affairs, we have some reason to hope that the Archduchess Marie Louise will be reduced to a considerable annual pension. I must tell Your Majesty that I am deeply interested in bringing this about, because by this means the name of Bonaparte would certainly be struck from the list of sovereigns, both now and for the future. The Island of Elba is his only for his lifetime, and the son of the Archduchess ought not to possess an independent state."

The Emperor of Austria defended his daughter's rights but feebly, and Prince Metternich occupied himself much more with Napoleon's sister Caroline than with Marie Louise, the daughter of his own sovereign. The man who showed most interest in her was the Czar. Alexander's chief ambition was to be thought a chivalrous prince, and he made it almost a point of honor to demand the execution of the treaty of Fontainebleau: he considered it a proof of his magnanimity. As in 1814 he had been the courtier of the Empress Josephine at Malmaison, so at Schoenbrunn he wished to be that of the Empress Marie Louise. This rôle of protector to Napoleon's two wives, two dethroned princesses, suited his generous nature. The Bourbons gave him no great pleasure. He thought them too infatuated about the antiquity of their family. Sometimes he reproached himself for not having preferred to them, if not Napoleon, at least the King of Rome. He made a parade of walking arm in arm with Prince Eugene de Beauharnais every day. This intimacy between the Czar and Napoleon's adopted son exasperated both the old French Royalists and the new ones. Talleyrand either considered or pretended to consider Alexander a frivolous and superficial person who loved a false popularity; a self-seeking apostle of a pretended liberalism. The ex-dignitary of the Empire had written to Louis XVIII. on November 12, 1814: "It is reported that the Emperor Alexander, in speaking of the Austrian opposition to his views, and after bitter complaints against M. de Metternich, said: 'Austria thinks itself sure of Italy, but there is a Napoleon there who could be made useful.' I cannot vouch for the truth of this, but the saying goes the rounds, and if it be true, it gives an exact measure of him who made it." Louis XVIII. replied, November 22: "I credit the speech attributed to the Emperor Alexander. It is of the highest importance, therefore, that Austria and England should take to heart the adage, trivial if you will, but full of sense, and specially applicable under existing circumstances, *Sublatâ causâ, tolliter effectus.*" The truth is, Talleyrand should have blushed to be the accuser of Napoleon when the Czar, in spite of the terrible memories of the Russian campaign, was his defender. The more averse he became to Austria, whose views were in opposition to his own, the more sympathy did Alexander show toward Marie Louise. He frequently went unannounced to Schoenbrunn, and lavished marks of the sincerest esteem and most exquisite courtesy on the dethroned sovereign.

Marie Louise, feebly defended by her father, was reduced to solicit in writing the good offices of the other monarchs. She addressed her petitions not only to the Czar, but to the King of Prussia. Lord Castlereagh presented himself at Schoenbrunn in boots and carrying a riding-whip, and only withdrew on being admonished that his costume was contrary to etiquette. The Minister probably thought that an Austrian Archduchess had forfeited her claim to polite treatment by the fact of becoming the Emperor Napoleon's wife. One might have said that the members of the Congress took a malicious pleasure in heaping up obstacles to the execution of the most solemn promises. The ink was hardly dry on the treaty signed at Fontainebleau, April 11, 1814, before its most precise stipulations were disregarded. No pains were taken even to find pretexts for excusing these violations of sworn faith. In this affair, as in that of Saxony, it must be owned that the sovereigns set a by no means good example to their people. It was they who undermined the bases of both throne and altar.

Prince Talleyrand wrote to Louis XVIII., February 15, 1815: " As to the territorial arrangements in

Italy, the commission charged with preparing the plan have proposed to give Parma, Piacenza, and Guastalla, to the Queen of Etruria; the Legations to the Holy See; the Presides, Piombino, and the reversion of Elba to the Grand Duke of Tuscany. The Archduchess Marie Louise would have nothing but a pension paid by Tuscany and certain fiefs formerly held by the old German Empire and now by the Grand Duke of Tuscany, to whom they were given as the completion of his indemnity by a decree of the Diet. They are situated in Bohemia, and yield an income of four hundred thousand florins. This scheme was presented through our influence. It has the double advantage of not merely diminishing the number of petty sovereignties in Italy, but, what is still more essential, that of sending the son of the Archduchess out of the way and depriving him of all expectation of ever reigning. Austria hesitated for a month, but the Emperor has at last decided to yield the duchies to the Queen of Etruria; he says it would not be becoming to keep either for himself or any of his family a state belonging to the House of Bourbon, with whom it is both his interest and his duty to remain on good terms. But, knowing that his daughter is determined to have an independent establishment, he has proposed that she shall have Lucca, and has charged his Minister to negotiate the affair with her."

Marie Louise was energetic in her refusal of this scheme, and Talleyrand added these sentences to his letter: "M. de Metternich presented this counter-project and discussed it with me before going to the Archduchess. His presumption and his excessive levity had prevented his foreseeing that it might not be a complete success. But at the first word, the Archduchess Marie Louise appeared unwilling to content herself with Lucca, and even not to care at all for that principality. She said it would not be agreeable to go there while Napoleon is at Elba. She insists, or, rather her advisers insist, on the rights secured to her by the treaty of April 11. She does not demand Parma, but she will have something equivalent or nearly so. I see no way to satisfy her, short of giving her the Legations, while securing their reversion to the Holy See. But the court of Rome, which cannot be reconciled even to the loss of Avignon, would make an outcry, and perhaps even resort to means of defence compromising to itself. M. de Metternich demands three days to consider his course of action, and will then give me his answer."

So then Talleyrand, who continued to wear the title of Prince of Benevento, stolen from the Pope, would have asked nothing better than to rob Pius VII. of the Legations. The obstinacy with which Marie Louise asserted her right to Parma prevented the success of this combination. But in order to obtain this duchy so much desired, she was at last wearied into a promise not to take her son there with her. The Duchy of Parma was the reward of all the bad actions suggested to her by the Mephistopheles of diplomacy. "Do you want to be Duchess of Parma?" was said to her; "abandon your husband forever; swear never to write him a single line. Do you want to be Duchess of Parma? Renounce your son also; you cannot enter your new dominions with this child. Leave him at Vienna. You may come to see him from time to time; but Parma is as much interdicted to him as France. You may be Duchess of Parma, Piacenza, and Guastalla, but only on one condition: your son shall not be your heir, but simply and absolutely an Austrian subject, or better, a prisoner."

However, the fêtes continued. The sovereigns cloaked their dissensions under a pretence of amusement. Lent put a stop to the balls, but all other dissipations went on as usual. On March 3, 1815, Talleyrand wrote to Louis XVIII.: "In the embarrassment of not knowing how to pass the time when dancing is given up, all sorts of games and amusements are resorted to. Among the most fashionable are lotteries, to which each person invited contributes a prize, so that there are no blanks, and every one wins. Day before yesterday Princess Marie Esterhazy gave a lottery of this description, and by an excess of civility which has been severely criticised, she undertook to arrange matters so that the four chief prizes should fall to women particularly distinguished by the Czar and the King of Prussia, both of whom were present. The scheme was frustrated by young Metternich, who approached the basket when it was not his turn and drew a ticket which was found to entitle him to the most magnificent lot of all: it had been brought by the Emperor of Russia. The latter was not able to hide his chagrin, and every one present was highly amused. Your Majesty will remember that the Czar does not attend M. de Metternich's balls of late nor speak to him when they meet elsewhere. The Emperor had nothing but illluck that evening. A prize which had been brought by the young Princess of Auersberg, for whom he seems to have a preference, was won by an aide-de-camp of the King of Prussia. The Emperor proposed an exchange, but the winner refused; the Emperor insisted, even to the point of claiming that it had been intended for him; the aide-de-camp replied that it was too precious for him to think of parting with it. All this delighted everybody, and it was quite enough to persuade the Emperor that the soirées at Vienna by no means display the good taste which marked them when he came."

On March 5, 1815, the Austrian Empress gave an evening party at which *tableaux vivants* were to furnish the entertainment. The principal one represented an interview between Maximilian I. and Marie of Burgundy. The most charming women of the court figured in it, and the spectators were still enjoying its unusual excellence when suddenly an unwelcome rumor began to circulate. Maximilian, Marie of Burgundy, the bishop, the ladies, the chevaliers, the Grand Mistress, — all the personages of the tableau seemed disturbed. On some faces there was anger, on others stupefaction. What news was it that produced this profound impression of surprise and terror? They had just learned that Napoleon had quitted Elba, and every one asked himself, "Where is he going?"

No more amusements, no more feasts! To arms! all Europe was about to cry. To arms all the troops of the Coalition! To arms a million of men against a battalion from the Isle of Elba! Napoleon breaks his parole. But the Bourbons, the Allies, had not they broken theirs? Not receiving the subsidy stipulated by the treaty of Fontainebleau, the Emperor was on the verge of famine. The moment was near when he would be obliged to disband his brave grenadiers, the companions of his glory, his consolers in misfortune. His wife and child had been torn from him. He was treated like a brigand. The intention to transport him like a vile criminal to some distant island of the Atlantic was openly avowed. Had not Talleyrand, the ingrate Talleyrand, written to Louis XVIII., on October 13, 1814: "There is a fixed resolve expressed to remove Bonaparte from Elba, but no one seems able to settle on a suitable place for him. I propose one of the Azores. It would be five hundred leagues from any country." Had not Louis XVIII., in his answer of October 21, spoken of that " *excellent idea of the Azores*"? And had not Talleyrand, writing again to the King, December 7, 1814, said: "We must hasten to get rid of Murat and the man of Elba"? Fatal as were the consequences of this return from Elba, which led to Waterloo, it must be owned that Napoleon had a right to defend himself against proceedings contrary to justice and morality. He was not merely a general seeking to replace himself at the head of his troops, a sovereign anxious to reconquer his sceptre; he was a husband and father bent on regaining possession of his wife and child.

VII.

THE RETURN FROM ELBA.

SATURDAY, *February* 25, 1815. The Island of Elba presents its customary aspect. No one has as yet the least notion of the resolution Napoleon is about to take. Nothing is talked of at Porto-Ferrajo but the ball to be given in the evening by the beautiful Princess Pauline Borghese, the Emperor's sister. This fête is very brilliant. All the officers are present, as well as the notabilities of the island and some visiting foreigners. Napoleon is very gay; his easy and cheerful conversation betrays no preoccupation. He stays until a late hour, and then takes Generals Bertrand and Drouot home with him to tell them his news from Vienna and France. At Vienna they have decreed his transportation to the Azores. In France the entire army and the majority of the people await him as a liberator. He says, "We will start to-morrow!"

Sunday, February 26. Bertrand and Drouot have kept the secret faithfully. The Emperor holds his levee as usual, and afterwards is present at the parade and at the Mass. Up to four in the afternoon the

troops know nothing. The roll of the drums summons them to dinner; and when that is over they
are ordered to repair to the wharf with their arms
and baggage. At five the signal for embarkation is
given, and some four hundred of the Guard, with
their officers, go on board the brig *Inconstant*, which
carries twenty-six guns. The remainder of the troops,
amounting to about seven hundred, embark on the
schooner *Caroline* and five other small vessels. The
wharf is full of people. The inhabitants bid an affectionate adieu to the soldiers whom they esteem and
love. Madame Mère and the Princess Pauline are
at the chateau windows. Napoleon appears and is
cheered, his countenance meanwhile beaming with joy
and confidence. He goes on board the *Inconstant*,
which is commanded by Captain Chautart with naval
Lieutenant Taillade as second officer. The flotilla
gets under sail with a south wind blowing. Night
falls; by daybreak they hope to have rounded
Capraja and to be beyond the French and English
cruisers which operate from that side. But hardly
have they doubled the Elban cape of Saint André
when the wind goes down and the sea becomes
absolutely calm.

Monday, February 27. Day breaks; they have
made only six leagues, and are in full sight of the
cruisers, between Capraja and Elba, chained, as it
.were, upon a moveless sea. Some of the naval officers
advise a return to Porto-Ferrajo. But the wind rises
again, and Napoleon orders the voyage to be con-

tinued. At four in the afternoon they are off the heights of Leghorn. One frigate is sighted five leagues to leeward; another is close to Corsica; and in the distance is seen a man-of-war approaching the flotilla with the wind astern. It is the *Zéphir*, a vessel of the French royal navy, commanded by Captain Andrieux. What is to be done? Shall they run up the tricolor and try to induce this officer to declare for Napoleon. The Emperor will not risk an imprudence which may not succeed. He orders the grenadiers to take off their foraging caps and hide under the bridge. At six in the evening the *Zéphir* and the *Inconstant* are near enough to speak, and a dialogue opens between Lieutenant Taillade and Captain Andrieux, who know and salute each other. The former takes his speaking-trumpet: —

"Where are you bound?"

"To Leghorn. And you?"

"To Genoa. Have you any commissions I can execute there?"

"Thanks, not any. How is the Emperor?"

"Very well."

"So much the better."

The conversation ends; the two vessels continue their opposite routes and lose sight of each other. The officer of the royal navy does not suspect that Cæsar and his fortunes have just passed by. The other vessels which had alarmed the imperial flotilla have disappeared from the horizon.

Tuesday, February 28. During the night the wind

has continued to freshen. At dawn a vessel of seventy-four guns is seen in the distance which appears to be going to Saint-Florent or Sardinia; but it soon becomes evident that it will not trouble itself about the Emperor's flotilla. They have been thirty-six hours at sea, and the soldiers do not yet know whither they are bound. All at once, Lieutenant Taillade notices that Captain Chautart has turned the vessel's head away from France. "Gentlemen," he says to the officers on the bridge, "are we going to Spain or to Africa?" Some one reports this to Napoleon, and he summons Taillade.

"Where are we?" he says.

"Sire, we are headed for Africa."

"I don't desire to go there. Take me to France."

"Your Majesty shall be there before noon tomorrow."

Then the Emperor, turning toward the soldiers of the Old Guard : —

"Yes, grenadiers, we are going to France, to Paris." And the soldiers break into enthusiastic cries.

Napoleon makes of the deck of the *Inconstant* both his promenade and his cabinet. While the wind blows and they near the coast of France, he dictates two proclamations, one to the people, the other to the army. "Frenchmen, in my exile I have heard your lamentations and your prayers; I have crossed the seas in the midst of perils of every kind; I arrive among you to resume my rights, which are also yours.

I will forget forever all that individuals may have said, done, or written since the taking of Paris, because there are events which are too powerful for human nature. Frenchmen, there is no nation, however insignificant, which has not had the right, and has not attempted, to free itself from the dishonor of obeying a prince imposed on it by a momentarily victorious enemy. When Charles VII. re-entered Paris and overthrew the ephemeral power of Henry VI., he recognized that he owed his throne to the valor of his soldiers and not to the Prince Regent of England. And it is to you alone, and to the brave men of the army, that I glory and will ever glory in owing all."

The proclamation to the army is more ardent still: "Soldiers, we have not been vanquished. Two men, risen from our ranks, betrayed our laurels, their country, their prince, their benefactor. Shall those whom we have seen for twenty years scouring Europe to make enemies for us; those who have passed their lives fighting against us in foreign armies and cursing our beautiful France ; shall they command and chain our eagles, they who never could endure their glance ? Shall we suffer them to inherit the fruit of our labors, to seize our honors and our goods and calumniate our glory? Should their reign endure, all would be lost, even the souvenir of our most memorable days."

Then, in a martial voice which grew more animated from phrase to phrase, Napoleon thus ended his dictation, sonorous as the note of a clarion : —

"Come, range yourselves beneath the banners of your chief. His existence is bound up with yours; his rights are yours and those of the people; his interest, his honor, his glory, are nothing but your interest, your honor, your glory. Our onset and our victory will march side by side; the eagle with the national colors will fly from steeple to steeple, till it reaches the towers of Notre Dame. Then you can show your scars with honor; then you can boast of what you have done; you will be the liberators of the fatherland."

As soon as the dictation is finished, the subaltern officers begin to transcribe it with so much zeal that five hundred copies are ready before they land.

Wednesday, March 1. In the morning they behold with joy the coast of France. At noon they sight Antibes and the Islands of Sainte-Marguerite; at three they anchor in the Bay of Juan. The guns of the *Inconstant* fire salvos of rejoicing, and every soldier dons his tricolored cockade. The boats are let down, and the landing is completed by five in the afternoon. They bivouac in an olive plantation near the shore. "Happy omen!" cries Napoleon; "the olive is the emblem of peace." He plucks some violets; then a table and chair are brought, and he sits down and spreads out his maps. He must choose between two roads, — that of lower Provence, which is easy, but where he cannot rely on the favorable attitude of the people, and that of Dauphiny, which bristles with rocks and mountains covered with ice and snow, but where they will encounter sympathetic sentiments. This route, too, will recall the passage of the Alps at the time of the Marengo campaign, and the Emperor settles on it. The moon rises. At eleven he leaves the bivouac and goes toward Cannes, whither he had sent General Cambronne with a vanguard to buy mules and horses. He passes through Cannes at midnight, and continues his route, leaving Antibes on the right.

Thursday, March 2. The Emperor has marched all night. At daybreak they wind round Grasse, and take up position on a plateau which overlooks the town. Some of the inhabitants bring provisions, which the Emperor accepts and pays for. After resting two hours, he sets off again in the direction of Sernon. At Grasse he abandons the four field-pieces which composed his artillery, because they would be impediments on the almost impassable roads they are about to traverse. A hundred men under Cambronne form the vanguard; the Emperor is in the centre, with the battalion of the Old Guard, which escorts the treasure and the ammunition and stores; the Corsican battalion form the rear-guard. The way is difficult and the cold severe. They march in single file along roads bordering precipices, down which several mules, one of them laden with gold, plunge and cannot be rescued. Napoleon, obliged to dismount in order to keep warm, more than once stumbles in the snow. Once he rests for a moment in a cabin where there is an old woman, and draws near her brushwood fire.

"Have you any news from Paris?" he says to the old peasant. "Do you know what the King is doing?"

"The King?" answers the old woman. "You mean to say the Emperor. He is always down yonder."

So the peasant has heard not a word of all that has happened in the last year. O vanity of glory! Napoleon looks pensively at General Drouot. "Well, Drouot," he says, "what is the good of troubling the world in order to fill it with our name?"

In the evening he arrives at Sernon, on the confines of the Department of the Lower Alps. He and his troops have marched twenty leagues that day. His soldiers are worn out with fatigue, but their enthusiasm revives them.

Friday, March 3. The Emperor, who passed the night at Sernon, resumes his march in the morning. The cold remains bitter, and the roads, covered with snow, continually ascend. The Polish lancers, who have not yet been able to obtain horses, carry their equipments on their shoulders. Nobody complains, and they cover almost as many miles as on the previous day. At night they sleep at Barême, ten leagues from the banks of the Durance.

Saturday, March 4. They make an early start, and at one in the afternoon the Emperor on horseback enters Dijon, where he breakfasts. At half-past three he gets into the saddle again, and departs, leaving General Drouot, with four grenadiers, to look after the printing of his proclamations, which until now have circulated in manuscript. At nine he reaches Malijai, where he sleeps.

Sunday, March 5. They turn towards Sisteron, where a great obstacle is to be dreaded. The fortress of this town is separated from the Durance by a bridge. What is to be done if it is defended, or its single arch blown up? But at two in the morning, General Cambronne and the advance guard reach the bridge and seize it unresisted. Napoleon enters Sisteron without difficulty, breakfasts, and receives the sub-prefect and the mayor, who come to pay their compliments, while the people give him an enthusiastic welcome. As his Arabian is too tired to go any further, he takes another horse, pursues his route, and sleeps that night at Gap.

Monday, March 6. The Emperor spent the night at Gap, with only ten cavalrymen and forty grenadiers. His advance guard had started several hours before him, for the purpose of exploring the dangerous defile of Saint-Bonnet, which, on leaving Gap, crosses a high mountain at the pass of Saint-Guignes, and connects the valley of the Durance with that of the Drac, one of the affluents of the Isère. Napoleon waits for the rear-guard, and leaves Gap with it at two in the afternoon. The whole population of the town turns out to see him go. They pass the defile without difficulty. At Saint-Bonnet, the inhabitants, seeing how few troops he has, tremble on his account; they beg him to sound the tocsin, and summon all able-bodied men in the surrounding villages for an escort. "No," says he; "your sentiments prove to me that I did not deceive myself. They guarantee the sentiments of my soldiery. Those whom I meet will range themselves on my side. The more of them there are, the more certainly will my success be assured. Stay quietly at home." Napoleon sleeps at Corps, a town on the boundary of the Department of the Isère, while his advance guard march all night toward the village of La Mure.

Tuesday, March 7. The solemn moment is approaching. As yet the Emperor has met no troops to bar his passage. The white flag and the tricolor have not found themselves face to face. Not a soldier belonging to the armies of Louis XVIII. has joined the little phalanx from the Island of Elba. No one can assure the Emperor that they will not fire on him. Even among the Bonapartists there are a good many officers who are unwilling to violate the oath so recently taken to the King. A terrible conflict goes on in their hearts between the memory of past glories and the sentiment of present discipline. If an officer orders a volley, will the soldiers obey? The whole question is there. Napoleon, daring as he is, and accustomed to risk all for all, has never, in his whole adventurous career, engaged in a more doubtful game. A little longer, and what will he be? A triumphant Cæsar, saluted by his legionaries, or a corpse riddled with balls? God alone knows.

In both camps the night of March 6–7 has been

full of anxiety. All the troops garrisoned in Dauphiny and the part of Savoy owned by France — that is to say, the 7th and 11th of the Line, the 3d Engineers, the 4th Artillery, and the 4th Hussars — are concentrated at Grenoble in order to arrest there him whom the Royalists call the Brigand of Elba. Toward midnight a battalion of the 5th of the Line meets the Polish lancers of the imperial advance guard at La Mure. Both expect a collision; but Lessard, the head of the battalion as well as the commander of the royal advance guard, orders his troops to turn back to Laffrey, a little village two leagues from La Mure and six from Grenoble, which it enters at five in the morning. On his part, Cambronne, commander of the imperial advance guard, who arrived at La Mure in the night, thinks it prudent to lead his men back to this side of Ponthaut, where he occupies the bridge.

At dawn Commandant Lessard finds himself at Laffrey, with a battalion of the 5th Line and a number of engineers and artillery-men, in a position between lakes and mountains very easy to defend.

At nine Napoleon is at Ponthaut, preparing for his onward march, with that imperturbable calm which he has never lost in the greatest crises and most formidable perils of his stormy destiny. He divides his little column into three bodies. Colonel Mallet takes command of the three companies forming the advance guard. The Polish lancers, under Colonel Jermanwski, take the right side of the road. The

officers who are without troops take the left, under
Major Pacconi. Napoleon, in the midst of the advance guard, on horseback, wearing the famous gray
overcoat and the broad ribbon of the Legion of Honor,
and attended by Generals Bertrand, Drouot, and
Cambronne, goes to meet the Royalist troops, who
have remained in position before Laffrey, between
the mountains and the lakes.

About one o'clock in the afternoon some Polish
lancers, who had been sent ahead to see how the
land lay, try to open a parley with the battalion of
the 5th Line. Commandant Lessard assures them
that if they renew the attempt he will fire on them.

Napoleon draws near. He descends from his
horse. "Tell the soldiers to put their weapons under
their left arms, points down," said he, to Colonel Mallet. "Sire," responds the Colonel, "is it not dangerous to act thus in presence of troops whose
sentiments we do not know, and whose first fire
may be so fatal?"

The Emperor repeats: "Mallet, tell them to put
the weapons under their arms." The order is executed. At the sides of the road mute and attentive
peasants watch the scene about to take place. The
two battalions are not more than a pistol-shot apart.
The silence is absolute: profound emotion almost
stops the breath.

Napoleon goes forward all alone. His legendary
profile defines itself against the sky. "Present
arms!" commands the head of the royal battalion.

The guns are levelled at the man of Austerlitz, who, impassible, continues slowly to advance. Arrived in front of the battalion, he raises his hand to his cap and salutes; then, in a strong voice: —

"Soldiers of the 5th," he cries, "do you recognize me?"

"Yes, yes," replies some one.

Then he adds: "Soldiers, behold your general; behold your Emperor. Let any one of you who wishes to kill him, fire!"

At these words the soldiers, instead of firing, throw themselves down on their knees. They kiss Napoleon's hands; they call him father; they utter frenzied acclamations. Their shakos wave from the tips of their sabres and bayonets. "Everything is over," said Napoleon to Bertrand and Drouot. "In ten days we shall be at the Tuileries."

The soldiers trampled under foot their white cockades, and put in their place the tricolored ones, which they had kept at the bottom of their knapsacks. Before taking up the march again, the Emperor has them drawn up in battle array, and addresses this allocution to them: "Soldiers, I come with a handful of brave men because I count on the people and on you. The throne of the Bourbons is illegitimate, because it was not erected by the nation; it is contrary to the national will, since it is contrary to the interest of our country, and only exists for the profit of certain families. Ask your fathers; question all these people who come here from the neighborhood; you will learn the real state of affairs from their lips. They are threatened with a return of the tithes, the privileges and rights of feudal times, and all the other abuses from which your successes had delivered them." At this moment a peasant cries out, "Yes, Sire; they wish to attach us to the soil. You come, like the angel of the Lord, to deliver us."

The troops, having fraternized, march on toward Grenoble, the Emperor at their head. The throngs of peasantry constantly grow larger, and join their shouts to those of the soldiery. They reach Vizille, where the enthusiasm of the inhabitants is excessive. "It is we," said they, "who first dared to reclaim the rights of man. This is the cradle of the Revolution; and it is here that French liberty revives again and France recovers her independence and her honor."

Between Vizille and Grenoble they see a regiment of infantry coming toward them. It is the 7th of the Line, commanded by Colonel de Labédoyère. He has left Grenoble to meet Napoleon. He has had the eagle of the regiment taken out of a chest, and, brandishing his sword and crying, "Long live the Emperor!" he had said, "Soldiers! Those who love me follow me!" The soldiers followed him. Napoleon and the Colonel get off their horses at the same moment and throw themselves into each other's arms. "Colonel," says the Emperor, "it is you who replace me on the throne."

The reunited troops, amounting to nearly three

thousand men, march to Grenoble escorted by several
thousand peasants. The Royalist authorities have
closed the gates of the city. The ramparts are covered by the 3d regiment of Engineers, consisting of
two thousand sappers, veterans whose bodies are fur-
rowed with glorious wounds; by the 4th Artillery, of
which the Emperor had been made captain twenty-
five years before; by two battalions of the 5th of the
Line; by the 11th of the Line and the Hussars of the
4th. Advancing before the ramparts, Labédoyère,
speaking in profound darkness, says: "Soldiers, it
is I, Labédoyère, Colonel of the 7th. We bring you
Napoleon. He is yonder. It is for you to receive
him and to repeat with us the rallying cry of the former conquerors of Europe: Live the Emperor!" The
troops on the ramparts respond by an immense shout.
Furious at finding the gates of the city closed, they
try to force them with axes, while, on the outside,
bands of peasants are busy in breaking them down.
Under this double strain they finally give way. It
is nine in the evening. Two human streams flow
against each other. Three thousand soldiers and
several thousand peasants who surround Napoleon
crowd upon the drawbridge at the risk of stifling
their sovereign in order to enter with him into the
city. Five thousand soldiers of the garrison and the
greater part of the inhabitants of Grenoble precipitate themselves toward the same point to meet the
Emperor. Flambeaux and torches illuminate this
scene, noisy with confusion and enthusiasm. It is

with great difficulty that Napoleon forces a passage through the delirious crowd and reaches an inn, the Three Dauphins, where he spends the night.

Wednesday, March 8. The Emperor stays all day at Grenoble. He governs there; he reigns. After receiving the city authorities he reviews the troops of the garrison. He ascertains with joy that in the twinkling of an eye these ten thousand men have resumed their tricolored cockades — cockades old and soiled; for when they were obliged to take them off, they had hidden them at the bottom of their knapsacks, hoping to put them on again some day. Some of the men, as they pass the Emperor, say: "This is the same we wore at Austerlitz." "This," say others, "we had at Marengo."

After the review Napoleon writes to Marie Louise, announcing his happy arrival at Grenoble and begging her to rejoin him with his son at Paris, where he expects soon to be. This letter is sent to General de Bubna, commander of the Austrian troops at Turin, who is requested to transmit it to the Empress.

Thursday, March 9. The Emperor, who slept at Grenoble, leaves the city at noon with a small army of six thousand men, and goes toward Lyons. His march is a long ovation. As he is fatigued, he travels slowly in an open carriage, surrounded by a crowd of peasants singing patriotic songs. "Ah!" says he, "I find here the sentiments which twenty years ago made me salute France as 'the great nation.' Yes, you are still the great nation. You will always be so." In the evening he sleeps at Bourgoin.

Friday, March 10. At Lyons the Royalists despair of arresting the Emperor's progress. The garrison, composed of the 13th Dragoons, and the 20th and 24th of the Line, will not remain faithful to the King in spite of the efforts of the Count of Artois and the Duke of Orleans. They had come from Paris to organize resistance, but they are obliged to take to flight. Marshal Macdonald has imitated them. The authorities have barricaded the bridge at the suburb of the Guillotière with pieces of wood, and drawn up troops upon the wharf. But the moment that they learn of the arrival of the Emperor, the soldiers destroy the barricade and throw the remains of it into the Rhone. Napoleon makes a triumphal entry into Lyons, where he installs himself in the Archbishop's palace.

Saturday, March 11. The Emperor reviews the troops in the Place Bellecour, and, directly afterwards, a division commanded by General Brayer sets off on its march toward Paris. Napoleon writes another letter to Marie Louise, announcing that he will be in his capital on March 20, the birthday of the King of Rome.

Sunday, March 12. The Emperor spends the day at Lyons in organizing his government. Satisfied with the dispositions of its inhabitants, he thanks them in these words : "Lyonnese, I love you."

Monday, March 13. He quits Lyons and sleeps at Mâcon.

Tuesday, March 14. He continues his route and goes to rest at Châlons-sur-Saône. The same day, at Lons-le-Saulnier, Marshal Ney, who was the sole hope of the Royalists, and who had, they say, promised Louis XVIII. to bring back Napoleon in an iron cage, declares for the imperial cause and makes a proclamation to his soldiers which opens thus: " The cause of the Bourbons is lost forever."

Wednesday, March 15. The Emperor sleeps at Autun.

Thursday, March 16. He rests at Avallon. On the same day Louis XVIII. holds a royal *séance* at Paris. He says to the Chambers: " I have once more seen my country; I have reconciled it with foreign Powers who will, I beg you to believe it, remain faithful to the treaties which have given us peace; I have labored for the welfare of my people; I have received, I receive every day, the most touching proofs of their affection. At sixty years, can I more worthily terminate my career than by dying in their defence? I fear nothing, then, for myself, but I fear for France. He who is coming to kindle among you the torch of civil war, brings also the scourge of foreign war; he comes to put our country once again beneath his iron yoke; he comes, in fine, to destroy that constitutional charter which I gave you, that charter which is my noblest claim to the esteem of posterity, that charter which all Frenchmen cherish, and which I swear to uphold. Let us rally about it then." While the King is yet speaking, a passing cloud wraps the hall in profound gloom. All eyes turn toward the ceiling to discover the cause of this sudden night. The emotion of the Royalists reaches its height, and, weeping, they cry: "Long live the King!"

Friday, March 17. Napoleon continues his march without obstacles, and passes the night at Auxerre.

Saturday, March 18. In this city he is rejoined by Marshal Ney. "Embrace me, my dear Marshal," he says to him. "There is no need to excuse yourself. Your excuse, like mine, is the course of events which have been stronger than men. Let us speak no more about the past, but think only how to retrieve the future."

The infantry embarks on the Yonne in time to reach Fontainebleau in the morning of March 20. The Emperor enters an open carriage with Bertrand and Drouot and drives thither.

Palm Sunday, March 19. At Paris Louis XVIII. has not yet announced his determination to take to flight. As usual, he assists at Mass in the chapel of the Tuileries. During the day he reviews his military household in the Champ-de-Mars. Between eleven o'clock and midnight, some travelling carriages are brought into the courtyard of the Tuileries and stop at the foot of the stairway of the Pavilion of Flora. Louis XVIII. comes down, and begins another exile. The weather is horrid and the night frightful. The rain falls in torrents; the wind, blowing in gusts, extinguishes the lights, which look like funeral torches.

During the day Napoleon has continued his march. *Monday-in-Holy-Week*, *March* 20. At four in the morning the Emperor arrives at Fontainebleau, where, exactly eleven months before, he had taken his memorable farewell of the Imperial Guard in the court of the Cheval-Blanc. Seeing this court once more; climbing the steps of the great stone stairway he had descended on April 20, 1814, without knowing whether he would ever remount them; entering the chamber where he had vainly sought in suicide a refuge against his mental sufferings, he experienced a sentiment of profound joy, and said to himself, "This is my revenge." At seven in the morning he receives from M. de Lavalette, who has just resumed the direction of the post-office at Paris, a despatch announcing the departure of Louis XVIII. He resolves to spend the night at the Tuileries to celebrate the birthday of the King of Rome.

What is happening at Paris? On awaking, the people do not yet know that Louis XVIII. has fled. From early morning crowds flock toward the Tuileries. A detachment of the National Guard is still at the palace, and the white flag is floating on the dome of the Pavilion of the Horloge. Some liveried domestics are in sight, but no body-guards. Soon the news of the King's flight is bruited about, and as the gratings of the palace are closed, some Bonapartists try to force them, but do not succeed.

At Saint-Denis the half-pay officers, who are warm partisans of the Emperor, assemble under the orders of General Exelmans. They persuade several detachments of infantry, a battery of artillery, and a squadron of cuirassiers to join them, and putting on the tricolored cockade, they march toward Paris. At two in the afternoon there they are, debouching into the Place of the Carrousel. At first the National Guard refuse to open the Tuileries to them, but they insist, and General Exelmans says that since the King is in flight and the entire army has declared for the Emperor, resistance will be useless. The gratings are opened, and the white flag on the Pavilion of the Horloge is replaced by the tricolor. General Exelmans and his soldiery, masters of the Palace of the Tuileries, wait there for Napoleon.

Almost at the same moment the Emperor at Fontainebleau gets into a carriage with Caulaincourt, Drouot, and Bertrand, and drives toward the capital, retarded somewhat by troops coming to rejoin him, and crowds of people who greet him with cries of joy.

At Paris the day is spent in waiting. Evening comes, and as the weather is bad, the crowds diminish. People go home to dinner. Everybody says: "It is late, and the Emperor will not come until to-morrow." However, the high officials of the Empire and their wives have come to the Tuileries, the men in uniform, and the ladies in full dress. The palace is illuminated as if for a fête. The lilies are torn from the tapestries and the bees reappear. Queen Hortense, King Joseph's wife, and the maids

of honor of Marie Louise are in the salons. Toward
nine o'clock they hear a great noise: it is the Emperor coming. Entering Paris by the Gate of Italy,
he has followed the exterior boulevards as far as the
Invalides, crossed the Pont de la Concorde, and gone
along the quay to the first gate of the Tuileries.
Frenzied acclamations resound on all sides, as his
carriage, surrounded by cavalry officers, enters the
courtyard of the palace. Inebriated with joy, mad
with enthusiasm, the half-pay officers fling themselves
before their sovereign, tear him from his carriage and
bear him on their arms, a living shield; kissing his
hands, embracing the skirts of his gray overcoat,
they drag him thus, in their delirium, to the foot of
the great stairway. It is only then that his feet are
permitted to touch the ground. The shouts redouble
until the very roof of the palace trembles with them.
Men press upon, they stifle each other. Two currents
meet on the stairway: one that descends to meet
Napoleon; one that tries to ascend the steps. The
Duke of Vicenza, who is behind the Emperor with
Bertrand and Drouot, recognizes Lavalette in the
crowd coming down from the first landing. "In
God's name," he cries, "get in front of him so that
he can proceed." Lavalette puts himself face to
face with Napoleon and going upstairs backward, one
step ahead of his master, succeeds in opening a
passage for him. "What! it is you," he says, "it
is you! it is you at last!" The Emperor sheds
tears of joy. He re-enters his chamber; last night

Louis XVIII. had occupied it. The prediction is accomplished. In twenty days, from the Bay of Juan, the imperial eagle has flown, without once stopping, from steeple to steeple, even to the towers of Notre Dame, even to the dome of the Palace of the Tuileries.

The next day, March 21, at one in the afternoon, Napoleon reviews in the Carrousel the soldiers who were at Paris, and the battalion from Elba, which had just accomplished a march that, for rapidity, has perhaps no parallel in history. Causing the officers of this battalion to approach, and showing them to the troops, the Emperor exclaims: "Soldiers, behold the officers who accompanied me in my misfortunes; all of them are my friends, all are dear to my heart. Each time that I saw them I seemed to see the army itself. Their presence recalled to me those immortal days which will never be effaced from your memories nor from mine. In loving them I love you. They have brought back to you, untouched and forever glorious, those eagles which for one moment treason had covered with a funeral pall. Soldiers, I give them back to you. Swear to me that you will follow them wherever the interests of our country call them." The soldiers answered, "We swear it." On the same day, the organizer of the republican armies, the famous Conventionist Carnot, is named Count of the Empire and Minister of the Interior.

On March 25, Napoleon again reviews the troops in the courtyard of the Tuileries. "How mad they

were," says he to them, " and how little they knew
the nation, who believed that Frenchmen would ever
consent to receive a prince from the same hands that
had laid waste our territory and, aided by treachery,
for a moment touched our laurels! The Bourbon
throne is as incompatible with the new interests of
the French people as it is with their glory. Soldiers,
I wish to give, in your presence, a special testimony
of my satisfaction with the brave garrison of Grenoble.
I know well that every French regiment would have
done as they did. So, too, I must avow my gratitude
to that courageous battalion of the 5th, and that
company of miners who, placed in a defile, came as
one man to surround their Emperor who had offered
himself to their fire. They have merited well from
the French nation, and from me and you." Interrupted by huzzas, Napoleon added only these words:
" Soldiers, you will be always faithful to the great
cause of the people, to the honor of France and to
your Emperor."

The next day, which was Easter Sunday, March 26,
Marshal Ney gave a dinner at Lille to the generals
and superior officers of the garrison. The following
toasts were drunk. By the Marshal: " To the Emperor Napoleon, our august sovereign! May this
name, cherished by the whole army, be forever the
rallying cry of all good Frenchmen! Live the Emperor!" By General Count d'Erlon: " To Her
Majesty, the Empress! On her return to us may she
find in the vivacity of our joy, the expression of the

love borne towards her by the French, and the regrets caused by her absence!" By General Duhesme: "To the Prince Imperial! May this august child, the source of so many hopes, long flourish under the guidance of his father, and inherit his great qualities for the welfare and the glory of France!"

On March 31, the Emperor visited the imperial institution of Saint-Denis, devoted to the education of the daughters of members of the Legion of Honor. He arrived unannounced. "It was a touching spectacle," said the *Moniteur*, "to see the Emperor surrounded by five hundred young girls whose fathers had either died on the field of battle or come back from it with honorable wounds. One understands the sentiment which made His Majesty say to the superintendent, 'You did not expect me ; but you might have known that my first visit would be to my imperial House of Saint-Denis.'"

At Paris, on Sunday, April 2, there was a grand military fête in the Champ-de-Mars, given by the Imperial Guard to the Parisian National Guard and the soldiers of the garrison.

About two in the afternoon nearly fifteen thousand men of all equipments dined in the open air on the Champ-de-Mars, the slopes of which were filled by an immense crowd. The bands played and the guests sang. The cry "Long live the Emperor!" broke in constantly like a refrain. In the galleries and salons of the Military School, the generals and other officers likewise sat down to a generous banquet. The bust of Napoleon was surrounded by emblems of victory. At dessert, when all present had drunk to the health of the Emperor, the Empress, and the Prince Imperial, and discharges of artillery were responding to the toasts, the guests, animated by a sudden and spontaneous movement, drew their swords from their scabbards, and waving them in air, renewed the oath to conquer or to die for their Emperor and their country. " To the column! to the column!" cried a voice, and the heroic crowd took up the cry. In the twinkling of an eye an immense procession of officers, soldiers, national guards and citizens were formed, and the bands of the Imperial Guard preceded them. An officer carried Napoleon's bust. They turned toward the Tuileries, and when they reached the garden, they stopped under the Emperor's cabinet windows and hurrahed for him until he appeared and thanked them. Then, going to the Place Vendôme, they hoisted the bust to the summit of the column, and encircled the pedestal with a garland of lights. The windows of every house in the square were at once illuminated as if by enchantment.

In his book on Lucien Bonaparte, Colonel Jung says: " The movement of 1815 was admirable for its ardor and patriotism. There is nothing like it in the history of France, except that of 1792, at the time of the departure of the volunteers for the frontier." And yet, despite so many testimonies of enthusiasm, Napoleon was melancholy. When the first intoxication of success was over, he doubted his good luck.

He was ill at ease in his new rôle as a constitutional monarch. What suited him was not liberty, but glory. He was like a lion who has let his claws be cut and his teeth pulled out, and to whom nothing but his mane is left. In his bureau drawers he found protestations of devotion addressed to Louis XVIII. by the very men who were now most vociferous in their cries of " Live the Emperor ! "

On March 8, Marshal Soult had written in an order of the day: " Bonaparte misapprehends us so much as to believe that we could abandon a legitimate and beloved sovereign in order to share the fate of a mere adventurer. He believes it, the madman ! His last act of lunacy serves to make him known." And now Marshal Soult was figuring in the first rank of the Emperor's courtiers.

In the *Débats* of March 19, Benjamin Constant had published an article in which these words occur: "He reappears at the extremity of our frontier, this man reddened with our blood and but lately followed by our unanimous maledictions. . . . Parisians, I have seen that liberty is possible under the monarchy; I have seen the King unite himself to the nation. I will not drag myself, a wretched renegade, from one power to another; I will not cover infamy by sophisms, nor stammer profane words in order to buy a shameful life." And now Benjamin Constant has accepted an appointment as Councillor of State from the Emperor. Napoleon is indulgent to all men who change their opinions; he has himself been by turns a Royalist, a Republican, an Imperialist, that is to say, an Emperor. Recantations and apostasies may afflict him, but his knowledge of the human heart is too profound for him to be astonished by them. It seems to him that France is an actress who, at every instant, changes her costume and her part without remorse. There is not time enough to tear off either the bees or the lilies from the escutcheons.

The functionaries who have just been resuming the tricolored cockade with so much zeal have probably taken care to hide the white one in a safe place, for sooner or later it is like enough to reappear. Oaths are taken only from the tip of the tongue; it is a simple formality. Napoleon knows all that; he knows also that Success is the god of France, and he says to himself anxiously, "Shall I succeed?" This immense Palace of the Tuileries, where he finds neither wife nor son, has lost its prestige for him, and is "only a sad and melancholy abode." In the depths of his soul he compares the 20th of March, 1815, with the 20th of March, 1811. The son's cradle has not been more solid than the father's throne. The child is exiled and proscribed. Now that the Pope has triumphantly re-entered the Eternal City, the title of "King of Rome" has an ironic ring. It was an infant's toy, this royalty of a day, and behold, the toy is broken. Napoleon may still be Emperor, but what has become of the crown of Italy, that iron crown, of which he had said so proudly under the vaulted roof of Milan cathedral: "God has given it to me; woe to him who touches it!" And the pompous title of Protector of the Rhine Confederation, what has become of that? Where are the German vassals of him who was but now a Charlemagne? How lugubriously they sound in the ears of a conqueror, those words, "Diminution, decadence!" Perhaps he recognized more fully at the Tuileries than he had done at Elba, his change of fortune; perhaps he is there more saddened by the clouds which hide the shining of his star.

VIII.

MARIE LOUISE DURING THE HUNDRED DAYS.

WHILE Napoleon, greeted by enthusiastic acclamations, was marching as a victor from Grenoble to the Tuileries, the cries of fury which
resounded against him in Vienna and throughout
all Germany never ceased to strike the ears of his
unfaithful spouse. It was not with pleasure that
Marie Louise learned that the Emperor had quitted
Elba, but with fear. Apprised of the news on coming
in from a walk, she seemed at first to ignore it. At
Schoenbrunn everything went on that evening just
as usual, — dinner, music, billiards. But the next
day, when the great event became known to the
French members of her household, it awakened
emotions so keen that one of the officials thought it
his duty to issue an order of the day prohibiting
all remarks upon the burning subject. Marie Louise
herself broke the silence. Her words betrayed the
trouble of her mind. She said the dangers which
the Emperor was incurring disquieted her extremely;
she was sure he would not succeed; her own situation

111

would become still more painful. Her uncle, the
Archduke John, Viceroy of Italy, is credited with
saying to her, "My poor Louise, I pity you; what
I should like for you and for us, too, is that your
husband should break his neck."

Nevertheless, the prisoner of the Coalition had
for a short time some inclination to better sentiments. When the Austrian Emperor was certain that
Napoleon had gone to France, and not to Italy, as
was at first believed, his anger moderated, and he told
his daughter that if, contrary to all expectation, her
husband should succeed, perhaps she would be permitted to rejoin him in case a pacific policy should
prevail. Then began an internal struggle in her
breast. According to M. de Méneval, the confidant
of her inward anxieties and fluctuations, she would
declare one day that she would never return to
France because she could see no hope of repose for
that country; on the next she would say that if her
husband renounced all projects of conquest and would
reign peacefully, she was convinced that no obstacle
would be interposed to her return, and she would
herself have no repugnance against it, because she
had always felt a liking for the French.

Napoleon's cause, then, was not absolutely despe-
rate at Vienna, at least during the early days of
March. But in making his calculations he had forgotten a Frenchman more pitiless toward him than
the most ruthless of the foreigners resolved on his
destruction. This was the man whom he had cov-

ered — nay, overwhelmed — with benefits; the ruined, unfrocked priest of whom he had made a minister, a prince, a great dignitary of the Empire. The same Talleyrand who had longed to exile his former sovereign to the Azores, bound up once more the fagot of the Coalition and reconstructed the Holy Alliance, despite the antagonism existing between the Cabinets of Vienna and Saint Petersburg. On March 13, 1815, the same day on which Napoleon, greeted with joy by the army and the people, left Lyons to continue his triumphant march to the Tuileries, his former Minister of Foreign Affairs had succeeded in obtaining the signatures of the Powers to the declaration of March 13 — that diatribe wherein he said, in most undiplomatic language, a medley of hate and terror: "In breaking the agreement by which he had been established at the Island of Elba, Bonaparte destroyed his sole legal title to existence. By reappearing in France, bent on projects of convulsion and dissension, he has proved, in the face of the universe, that there can be neither peace nor truce with him. The Powers declare, in consequence, that Napoleon Bonaparte is placed outside of all relations, both civil and social, and that, as an enemy and disturber of the peace of the world, he is handed over to public vengeance." The day after, Talleyrand wrote thus to M. de Jaucourt concerning this savage document, a sort of encouragement to assassination, whose violence the Powers themselves speedily regretted: "My dear friend, I send the King the declaration of which I spoke yesterday. It is very strong; no document of such force and importance has ever been signed by all the sovereigns of Europe."

On the same day, March 14, Talleyrand addressed the following paper to Louis XVIII. It was printed at Vienna, and spread broadcast throughout Germany, under the title, *Warning to the Nations :—*

"Bonaparte no longer desires to reign save for the welfare of the Jacobins. He contents himself with the actual boundaries of France, and proposes to live in peace with the rest of Europe. As surety he offers: 1st. The grapeshot wherewith he destroyed the Sections of Paris. 2d. The poisoning of the hospitals in Egypt. 3d. The assassination of Pichegru. 4th. The murder of the Duke of Enghien. 5th. The oaths taken to the French Republic. 6th. His repeated assaults upon all the governments of Europe. 7th. The spoliation of churches in Russia and Spain. 8th. His escape from Elba. 9th. The organization of three thousand battalions of the National Guard to replace the conscription. 10th. The violation of every treaty he has signed, including that of Fontainebleau. 11th. The abolition of collective rights in favor of public enthusiasm."

At this very time there was circulating in Germany a work by Maurice Arndt, entitled a *Catechism for German Soldiers and Military Men*, in which instructions were given concerning the duties of a Christian warrior. Its sixth chapter ran thus:—

"Concerning the Great Tyrant.

"And the abyss is open, saith the Lord, and hell has vomited its poison and set free its venomous serpents.

"And a monster is born, an abomination soiled with blood has risen up.

"And his name is Napoleon Bonaparte, a name of desolation, a name of woe, a name of malediction for widows and orphans, a name which will resound at the day of judgment amid outcries of despair.

"And yet many have adored him, and made him the idol of their soul; they have named him the Saviour, the Liberator, the Man who comes in the name of the Lord to redeem the world.

"And yet I know him not, saith God; I have reproved him and I will reprove him, and there shall be in him neither felicity, nor salvation, nor liberty.

"But he has become powerful by lying; he has built up his throne by murder and by treachery; and it is a sign of the times, and the mark of the sins of the children of men, and it proves how far they have wandered from the way of justice, that they have called it deliverance from oppression.

"Arise, ye peoples! Slay him, for I have cursed him; destroy him, for he is the destroyer of liberty and law."

This appeal to murder proves to what a pitch of hatred German wrath had risen against the man returned from Elba. Marie Louise heard nothing but imprecations against her husband, and the Germanic sentiments of her childhood and early youth awakened anew, and, perhaps, in her own despite, in the depths of her soul. On March 12, the eve of the declaration of the Powers, she caused General Neipperg, who constantly grew more influential with her, to write to Prince Metternich that she had no part in Napoleon's projects, and placed herself under the protection of the Allies. From that moment she decided irrevocably never to return to France.

Napoleon, on the other hand, was striving with all his might to regain possession of his wife and son, whom he was awaiting at Paris with extreme impatience. The Duke of Vicenza, his Minister of Foreign Affairs, tried in vain to renew relations with the Powers, and especially with Austria. General Baron de Vincent, who represented Vienna at the Court of Louis XVIII., demanded his passport on March 22. Nevertheless, he consented to have a secret and private interview with the Duke of Vicenza at the house of Madame de Souza before leaving Paris. The Duke tried in vain to plead his master's cause. All he could obtain was that one of the secretaries of the Austrian Embassy, M. de Rechtembourg, who was going to Vienna, should carry thither two letters from Napoleon, — one to his wife, and the other to his father-in-law, — also a letter for Prince Metternich. These letters reached their destination. But, being submitted to the Congress, they were as barren of results as had been those addressed to Marie Louise from Grenoble and Lyons by her husband.

Meanwhile an unceasingly annoying vigilance was exercised over the few French attendants who remained near the former Empress. All communication with France was rigorously interdicted; not even a French newspaper reached Vienna. The iron ring tightened daily about Marie Louise — for that matter, she had become the accomplice of her jailers.

On March 20, 1815, the very day on which Napoleon re-entered the Tuileries to celebrate there the birthday of the King of Rome, the child was torn from the arms of his governess, the virtuous and devoted Countess of Montesquiou, who had never quitted him since the hour when he came into the world, and who had always given him the care and affection of a mother. Talleyrand wrote thus to Louis XVIII. on that date: —

" SIRE: The Emperor Francis has just ordered Madame de Montesquiou to deliver up to him the child whom she has had in charge. Her language under existing circumstances has been so opposed to the resolutions taken by Austria and the other Powers, that the Emperor is unwilling to permit her to remain any longer near his grandson. To-morrow she should receive the order to return to France. The child will live in the palace at Vienna, where he will be guarded from the abduction which certain circumstances have made it seem probable will be attempted."

Madame de Montesquiou's crime in the eyes of the implacable Coalition was to have remained faithful to her benefactor; to have continued to speak of the great Napoleon before the little one ; to have said to the child, morning and evening, " Monseigneur, pray for your father." The despair of *Mamma Quiou*, as the King of Rome called her, was very great. She obliged her persecutors themselves to give proofs of their esteem for her. In protesting against the violence which deprived her of the functions she had fulfilled with so much zeal, she obtained a written order from the Emperor Francis, and a medical certificate attesting that she left her pupil in perfect health. But she demanded in vain that the Vienna *Gazette* should publish a formal denial of the pretended plot for carrying off the young Prince, which had been attributed to her son, Colonel Anatole de Montesquiou.

At this moment there was a person of whom Marie Louise was thinking much more than of her husband or her son. It was General Neipperg, who was preparing to go to war with Murat, who had once more become the ally of France and Napoleon. Furious at having been juggled with by Austria, which, after guaranteeing him his throne, had declared for a restoration of the Bourbons, he had sincerely repented of his conduct. On December 7, 1814, his representative at Vienna, the Duke of Campo-Chiaro, had remitted to Prince Talleyrand a note in these terms: " The King of Naples was a party to the Coalition whose efforts and success have placed Louis XVIII. on the throne of France ; his adhesion to this Coalition was not without utility to the common cause. The King of Naples has the right, therefore, to expect amicable relations with the house of Bourbon for which he finds that he has contended. Austria stipulated not only for itself, but for the Allies in the treaty concluded May 30, 1814, and the King of Naples had a solemn treaty with Austria which was known to all Europe."

Murat very soon understood that he had made a mistake in abandoning his brother-in-law and the French, companions of his exploits. The Princess Pauline Borghese, arriving at Naples from the Island of Elba, reconciled him with Napoleon, and ever since November, 1814, he had said of the eleven hundred soldiers the Emperor had with him there, " They are the nucleus of five hundred thousand." On March 24, 1815, he wrote to Napoleon : " I learn with inexpressible joy that Your Majesty has landed on the shores of the Empire. I should have been glad to have received some instruction concerning the co-operation of my movements in Italy with yours in France. . . . Sire, I have never ceased to be your friend. I simply waited for a favorable occasion. It has come, and now I am going to prove that I was always faithful, and to justify in your eyes and in those of all Europe, the opinion you conceived of me. On any other occasion, I should have sacrificed myself in vain."

When General Neipperg left Vienna, on April 1, 1815, to begin the war with Murat, Napoleon's ally, Marie Louise, whose sympathies were no longer French, certainly desired the success of Austria, and especially of the Austrian general. He wrote voluminous letters to her who had ceased all correspondence with her husband. The Machiavelian policy of the Coalition had borne its fruits. Neipperg was the counsellor, the confidant, the future minister, the future morganatic husband of the former Empress of the French. She was going to be — admitting that she was not so already — enthralled, body and soul, by this man, who, everywhere and always, from Sweden to Naples, had figured among the most persevering and most relentless of Napoleon's enemies.

However, Napoleon did not yet despair of recalling his wife to better sentiments. A few days after General Neipperg's departure, a mysterious envoy from Paris arrived at Vienna to make a supreme effort. One of the chief familiars of Prince Talleyrand had been a M. de Montrond, a man of the world, subtle, charming rather than serious, and more accustomed to the society of drawing-rooms than to politics. As he was both shrewd and witty, his opposition and his sarcasms incurred the Emperor's anger, and he had imprisoned him in the fortress of Ham. He made his escape, however, and found a refuge in exile, whence he returned to France at the same time with the Bourbons. After the return from Elba he made advances to Fouché, Napoleon's Minister of Police, who resolved to employ him in the hope of thus continuing relations with Prince Talleyrand. Who could have believed that M. de Montrond was to be the man whom the Emperor would charge with the most delicate and important secret mission. But as Napoleon desired at any price to see once more his wife and son, he would have accepted the services of any one whatever who seemed likely to aid him in realizing this dearest of his wishes.

M. de Montrond entered Vienna with a passport describing him as an Italian abbé; preserving a strict incognito, he had secret interviews with Talleyrand (whom he found more deeply pledged to the Bourbon cause than he had supposed), and afterwards with M. de Méneval. To the latter he delivered a letter for Marie Louise from Napoleon, and others written by the Duke of Vicenza to Madame de Montesquiou and to M. de Méneval himself. "He told me, laughing," says Méneval, "that he was authorized to abduct the Empress, disguising her in men's clothes if necessary, and not to mind her roguish ways. He made several other remarks in the same vein of witty raillery which is characteristic of him, and which proved to me what I was quite disposed to believe, that this abduction scheme was a jesting notion of his own rather than the object of his mission. He was surprised at the unexpected confidence placed in him at Paris, whence he had been hunted and exiled. I was surprised myself, for it seemed to me much more likely that he came to work for M. de Talleyrand than for the Emperor; as a matter of fact he had a secret mission from the Duke of Otranto for that minister. He stayed at the palace of the French Embassy."

To this strange envoy M. de Méneval gave several meetings, sometimes at Vienna, sometimes at Schoenbrunn. There Fouché's agent, strolling through gardens and greenhouses, passed as an amateur in botany, in order to put off their guard the many spies surrounding the residence of Marie Louise.

In a letter addressed to Louis XVIII., on April 13, 1815, Talleyrand thus expressed himself concerning M. de Montrond's secret mission : —

" All that reaches me from France proves that Bonaparte is greatly embarrassed there. I am still more convinced of it by the emissaries whom he sends here. One of these, M. de Montrond, has reached Vienna through the intervention of the Abbé Altien, an *attaché* of the Austrian legation at Paris. He has neither a despatch nor any ostensible mission, and possibly was sent by those who serve Bonaparte rather than by Bonaparte himself. This is what I incline to believe. He brought verbal messages to M. de Metternich, M. de Nesselrode, and me. His business was to ascertain whether the foreign Powers were seriously determined not to recognize Bonaparte and meant to make war against him. He had also a letter for Prince Eugene. What he was told to ask me was, whether I could really intend to excite war against France. Read the declaration by which I answered him. It does not contain a word contrary to my opinion. Moreover, it is not a war against France which is in question, but simply one against the man of the Island of Elba. Of M. de Metternich he inquired whether the Austrian government had totally lost sight of the ideas it held in March, 1814. 'The regency? We don't want that,' answered M. de Metternich. Finally he endeavored to find out the intentions of the Emperor Alexander through M. de Nesselrode. 'Bonaparte's destruction and that of his family,' said the latter. And there things rest. M. de Montrond has been made acquainted with the condition of the forces to be immediately employed, and also with the treaty of the 25th of March last. He has gone back to Paris with this information and these responses, which ought to give those who are at present attached to Bonaparte's fortunes a good deal to think about."

M. de Montrond took back to Paris a letter to the Duke of Vicenza from M. de Méneval, dated April 7, 1815. Among other items of news, M. de Méneval gave Napoleon's Minister of Foreign Affairs some painful and singular details concerning the sentiments of Marie Louise: "I do not know when the Empress will go to France," said the faithful servitor. "At present the Cabinet is far from being inclined to permit it. The mind of the Empress is so disturbed that the prospect of returning thither fills her with terror; for six months every possible means has been employed to detach her from the

Emperor. . . . When by accident I have been able to get a word with her, I have implored her to remain neutral and to sign nothing. But she has been induced to take several occasions to declare her igno‑ rance of the Emperor's plans and her wish to place herself under the protection of her father and his allies."

In the same letter M. de Méneval gives an account of a conversation he has just had with the forgetful Princess : " Last Sunday, dining alone with the Empress, Her Majesty said to me, after dinner, that the Congress had just signed an act assuring the Duchy of Parma to her, but leaving for the present the administration of it to Austria which should make it pay her one hundred thousand francs a month. She said she had not been able to obtain the inheritance of the duchy for her son ; her heir must be the son of the Queen of Etruria ; but that she will obtain the Bohemian fiefs of the Archduke Ferdinand, which yield a revenue of about six hundred thousand francs ; also, that she had taken an irrevocable determination never to be reunited to the Emperor. Pressed concerning the motive of this singular resolution, after several reasons which I undertook to set aside, she avowed that as she had not shared his disgrace, she could not share a prosperity she had done nothing to bring about. . . . While waiting for this tangle to get smoothed out, I went on talking to her about the happiness which had been caused in France by the Emperor's return, the impatience

with which she is expected there, and the desire the
Emperor has to see her; but I spoke soberly, for the
subject annoys her. All must be left to time and the
Emperor's moderation. No matter how prudently I
act, I am subjected to the basest espionage. A swarm
of ignoble spies prowl about me and comment on every
gesture, movement, and expression of countenance.
I fear I shall not be retained here much longer;
I need to breathe a different air and to see you
all; my health is impaired. No one but the Empress
and her son enjoy brilliant health. The Empress
has grown much stouter; the Prince Imperial is an
angel of beauty, strength, and sweetness. Madame
de Montesquiou sheds tears about him every day."

In a postscript dated April 8, M. de Méneval added:
"I have written you hastily and without order. I
have a thousand other things to tell you which it
would take too long to write. What I presume to
recommend you to be most circumspect about is that
which relates to the person of the Empress. This
Princess is really good-hearted, but at present she is
dominated by foreign influences."

Napoleon insisted on seeing the original of this
letter. It is easy to understand how greatly it must
have pained him.

Marie Louise was all the more culpable because,
had she acted in conformity with her duties as wife
and mother, as Frenchwoman and Empress, she
might have secured, if not the reconciliation of her
husband with the Powers, at least the accession of

her son. Even the bitterest enemies of her husband, as, for example, Benjamin Constant, had rallied to him. Many people considered the cause of the Bourbons as forever lost. At Ghent, French emigration was frequently discouraged. On March 27, M. de Jaucourt wrote to Talleyrand: "I am no longer good for anything; do not give me any mission; I want none. A little intrigue is all anybody is going to have to do outside the Congress, if that continues, and we are already assuming an appearance of emigration which I find odious." And again on April 11: "Nothing is so easy as to ruin and devastate France and bring about a revolution in its government; nothing is so difficult as to save it, to put it back where it was on the morrow of the royal meeting. Great God! what a road we have passed since that time."

Hostilities had not yet begun. Notwithstanding the declaration of March 13, the violence of which was already regretted, Europe felt a certain hesitation to reopen strife. In England a strong opposition had declared itself against the warlike attitude of the Ministry toward France, and the Cabinet was obliged to conceal from Parliament the treaty of March 25, by which the Powers had renewed their treaty of Chaumont. In spite of what Talleyrand had written to Louis XVIII., neither Austria nor even Russia would have absolutely repelled the idea of a regency under Marie Louise. If this Princess had cordially pleaded the cause of her husband and her son, if she

had made an ardent appeal to the chivalrous sentiments of the Czar, the Bourbons would probably
never have remounted the throne.

Alexander had been very indignant when he
learned that a secret treaty against him had been
signed during the Congress by England, Austria, and
France. He considered it an act of monstrous ingratitude on the part of Louis XVIII., for it was he who
had given him the crown of France some months
before; there would have been needed but a word to
make him proclaim Napoleon II., under the regency
of Marie Louise. It was Madame de Krudener, in
her rage at having been disdained by Napoleon not
long before, who decided the Emperor Alexander,
the white angel, as she styled him, to declare against
the man whom she called *the black angel*. Jacob, the
bibliophile, in his curious book on the Czar's Egeria,
says: " It cannot be denied that Madame de Krudener
had a most fatal influence upon the destiny of the Emperor Napoleon. It was she who first proclaimed the
decadence of *Buonaparte*, as she affected to name
him; it was she who, as if speaking in the name of
God, boldly declared that Napoleon had ceased to
reign and was about to be placed under the ban of
the nations; it was she, in fine, who, bringing all her
influence to bear on the hesitating Alexander, caused
the negotiations of Fontainebleau to be broken off
and decided the re-establishment of the Bourbons.
She publicly announced, in her Biblical phraseology,
that men would presently see the Revolution, war,

and every woe, proceeding from the Island of Elba with *the black angel,* who would unloose all these scourges upon Europe."

Nevertheless, the Emperor Alexander, opposed by France and Austria in his designs on Poland, and not less irritated against Talleyrand than against Metternich, may have more than once regretted having followed the advice of Madame de Krudener. When proclaimed by an unfrocked bishop, who had been a minister both of the Directory and the French Empire, the dogma of legitimacy produced no effect on the mind of Alexander. The Czar made no secret of his opinion that the suppression of the tricolored flag was a mistake. He approved the principles of the Parisian liberals. He accepted the idea of a monarchy under the Duke of Orleans almost as if he foresaw the Revolution of 1830, to which his successor, the Emperor Nicholas, was, nevertheless, to be so hostile: Guinguenée wrote to him, apropos of the return from Elba: "The execution of the plan has been marvellous. It was accomplished as much by the absence of resistance as by the calm yet swift audacity of the attack. Oppressed, humiliated, dishonored by the Bourbons, France has received Napoleon as a liberator. He alone can rescue it from the abyss. What other name is there to take the place of his? Let those of the Allies who are most capable of reflection, reflect on this, and try in good faith to answer the question."

The Czar experienced a secret antipathy towards

the Bourbons of the elder branch. We desire no better proof of this than a curious letter from Talleyrand to Louis XVIII., which bears date April 23, 1815, and may be found in the interesting collection published by M. Pallain. In it Talleyrand thus enumerates the Czar's grievances against the King: "For some time past I have had occasion to remark that if the Emperor of Russia often opposes what Your Majesty wishes, it is not always solely in view of some end which he is aiming at himself; but still more, in certain circumstances, because he feels wounded: First, because Your Majesty did not offer him the blue ribbon, as well as the Prince Regent; second, on account of the futility of his intercession for the Duke of Vicenza, in whom he was warmly interested, and who was excluded from the Chamber of Peers; third, on account of the firmness with which Your Majesty, on the question of marriage, refused to yield to his wishes on the religious point; fourth, because the constitutional charter differs on many points from the views he expressed in Paris on the subject, and which his attachment to liberal ideas made him consider very useful and very important."

In the same letter Talleyrand reports a conversation which had just taken place between the Emperor Alexander and Lord Clancarty: "Our first duties," said the Czar, "are towards Europe and ourselves. Even were the re-establishment of the King's government easy, yet, so long as there can be no certainty of its future stability, what should we do in re-establish-

ing it except to prepare new afflictions for France
and Europe? If what has happened once should
happen again, should we be as united as we are
to-day? Should we have nearly a million of men
under arms? Should we be ready at the moment
when danger impended? And what probability is
there, the elements of disorder remaining the same,
that the government of the King would be more
stable than it has been? In a word, whatever opinion one may have about it, since the re-establishment of the King, which we all desire, and which
I desire particularly, may meet with insurmountable
obstacles, therefore, this case being possible, it is good
to look ahead and agree beforehand what should then
be done."

The Emperor of Russia added, when speaking of
a possible imperial regency, this significant remark,
which greatly increases the responsibility of Marie
Louise for the fall of the Napoleonic dynasty: "Last
year the regency might have been established; *but
the Archduchess Marie Louise, to whom I spoke about
it, will not at any price whatever return to France.*
Her son is to have an establishment in Austria, and
she desires nothing further for him. I am certain,
moreover, that Austria, on its part, no longer dreams
of a regency or wishes for it. Last year it seemed to
me as if that might have conciliated the different
interests, but the situation is no longer the same. So
that is a thing which need not be considered. I see
nobody more likely to conciliate all than the Duke

of Orleans. He is a Frenchman, he is a Bourbon, and the husband of a Bourbon; he has sons; when he was young he served the Constitutional Cause; he has worn the tricolored cockade which, as I often said at Paris, ought never to have been given up."

In the same letter Talleyrand was not afraid to write to Louis XVIII.: "The Emperor Alexander said in ordinary conversation, that he could readily believe that Your Majesty, if you were alone, might suit France and be loved and respected there; but, as you cannot be separated from those surrounding you, he fears that you will never be able to consolidate your throne."

From this letter it clearly appears that the Emperor Alexander declined to be the defender of Marie Louise against her own wishes, and returned reluctantly to the elder branch of the Bourbons. They had shown him little gratitude, and yet, as is incontestably known, they could never have reascended the throne if it had pleased him to oppose his veto to their restoration. But Fatality weighed thenceforward on the man whom Fortune had once covered with her favors. His wife, instead of serving him, was prejudicial to him. The former Empress, the former Regent, had disappeared to give place to the Duchess of Parma. The marvellous return from Elba had left her indifferent, and even hostile. One would have said she was ashamed to appear again in the great drama wherein she had played a leading part.

The last ties, so feeble in any case, which might still have attached Marie Louise to France, were weakening every day. Her little French court was almost dispersed. Her lady of honor, Madame de Brignole, who had been so devoted to Napoleon, died on April 2. When the Emperor formed the household of Marie Louise, in 1810, he appointed as one of the ladies of the palace the Marquise of Brignole-Sale, then called the Countess of Brignole, as the title of Marquis had been abolished by the Emperor. A member of one of the most illustrious Genoese families, the nobility of her character, and her upright and distinguished mind placed her among the very small number of women with whom the Emperor willingly conversed on serious matters, and even on questions of policy. When the allied troops entered Paris, she used every effort to induce the Regent not to leave the capital; and, despite her chagrin at seeing her advice rejected, she followed Marie Louise to Vienna. When she fell ill there, the Empress gave her the most assiduous care, and wept for her as if she had been her mother. On her death-bed Madame de Brignole once more implored Marie Louise to rejoin Napoleon.

The Countess of Montesquiou, after having been violently separated from her pupil, was confined in a small apartment of two rooms at Vienna, and neither she nor her son, Colonel Anatole de Montesquiou, were permitted to return to Paris. On the other hand, M. Balkouhey, the intendant of the household, was authorized to do so. Baron de Bausset was confined to his bed with gout. Baron de Méneval alone remained near Marie Louise, and he for a short time only, and against his inclination. He longed to terminate his stay at Schoenbrunn, where all his efforts in behalf of a husband and father had been so fruitless. The type of honor and fidelity, this loyal adherent had neglected no means to recall Marie Louise to sentiments of duty. The journal which he kept at Schoenbrunn in 1814 and 1815 has been shown to me by his son. It is a very curious document. It contains nothing but facts without reflections, like the journal of Dangeau; but if it is read with attention, it gives a thorough knowledge of the attitude of Marie Louise and her mode of life. The name of General Neipperg recurs constantly in this journal. Every day the same things are recorded of the Empress: she rides with the General; she dines with the General; she plays or sings with the General. The word *factotum* comes in like a refrain. The seducer is perhaps still more influential when absent than when present. On April 1, 1815, occurs this entry: "General Neipperg left this morning at six. The Empress, who rose and dressed very early, learned his departure from a long letter which he left for her." On April 21: "The Empress received a letter from General Neipperg, dated at Modena, on the 14th. The Parmesan body-guards, having been unwilling to march against the Neapolitans, and several of them having cried 'Long live the Emperor!' this

company was disbanded.   At Parma the Empress
herself will reward those who remained faithful." So
what Marie Louise most desired was that the soldiers
of her duchy should oppose her husband. And when,
on May 2, the unfortunate Murat, who, as Napoleon
remarked, twice ruined France — once by abandoning
her, and again by returning to her too soon — was
completely beaten by the Austrians at the battle of
Tolentino, the Empress Marie Louise was the person
who rejoiced most over General Neipperg's success.
During his absence she had heard a piece of news
which apparently did not afflict her : it announced
the death of the General's wife. On this subject M.
de Méneval says : " The death of the Countess Neipperg passed unnoticed except at Schoenbrunn, where
it excited keen interest. This lady had remained
at Würtemberg, where General Neipperg originated
when he came to Vienna to seek employment for his
talents. She died in April, after two days' illness,
leaving four boys. They say she was very pretty,
but not very intelligent. Count Neipperg had abducted her from her husband, who was still living a
few months before his wife's death. The manner in
which the Empress Marie Louise announced this
death one morning at table was not indicative of
much regret."

The strange affection felt by Napoleon's wife for
General Neipperg overpowered every other sentiment. She had so absolutely disowned France and
her husband, that when the processions for the suc-

cess of the war began in Vienna on April 16, her step-mother, the Austrian Empress, had no scruples about asking her to take part in them. It is true that she refused compliance with an invitation so humiliating that even her father and her uncles saw the impropriety of it. In mentioning the fact, M. de Méneval adds this sorrowful reflection: " The Empress Marie Louise manifested sentiments appropriate to her position; but it costs me much to admit that she seemed to act in this way chiefly to preserve her right to persevere in her refusal to go back to France."

The faithful and loyal Méneval had lost all hope of winning back Marie Louise to better sentiments. The last interview he had with her on this painful subject robbed him of all illusions. She would not return to France for any consideration whatever, even if the Allies and her father should grant her their permission. "Some words," he says, "were exchanged between us on the painful subject of her refusal to rejoin the Emperor. She replied with some vivacity, but yet with her usual sweetness, that her resolution was irrevocable. When I objected that there was no such thing as an irrevocable resolution, and that some circumstance might occur which would render her return to France obligatory, she was in haste to reply that her father himself would have no right to force her. The remark escaped me that the sentiments that she was expressing were unjust and out of keeping with her character; that if the French nation were made aware of this repugnance, they would be wounded by it, as they were extremely sensitive when their attachment was disdained, and would then reject her, although they had desired her presence as a pledge of peace. This conversation was the last I had with her on this matter."

Even to have abandoned her husband was not enough for Marie Louise. She allowed her son to bo taken from her. She and the little Prince no longer lived under the same roof. She remained at Schoenbrunn, while the child was at Vienna, in his grandfather's palace. She knew that when she should go to reign in Parma, that duchy which was to be hers for life only, she would have no right to take the little Prince there with her. And yet the Duchy of Parma was like the Promised Land to her, because she was certain that her favorite would be at her side. This man's love outweighed all things else.

M. de Méneval comprehended that his presence at Schoenbrunn had become worse than useless. He requested his passports for France on April 9, and had been waiting for them nearly a month. Before taking his departure he went to the imperial palace at Vienna to bid adieu to the Prince, and was struck by the child's serious and melancholy air. His charming gaiety and graceful loquacity had given place to constraint, embarrassment, and timidity. He cast uneasy glances about him. His precocious sadness — he was a little more than four years old — almost persuaded one that he had already a presentiment of his sorrowful destiny. "Monseigneur," M.

de Méneval said to him, "I am going to see your
father again. Have you any messages for him?"
The child, as if he felt himself surrounded by evil-
disposed persons, remained silent; withdrawing his
hand from that of his father's faithful servant, he
went without speaking to the embrasure of the far-
thest window. Then he beckoned Méneval to approach, and said in a whisper, "Monsieur *Méva*, tell
him that I always love him well."

On May 6, at ten in the evening, M. de Méneval took leave of the Empress Marie Louise. This
woman, ordinarily so unmoved, could not avoid
yielding to a brief emotion. Possibly a secret remorse agitated the depths of her soul. After saying
a few courteous words to this high-principled man,
whose noble counsels had been, alas! of so little
avail, she expressed herself nearly in these words:
"I feel that all relations between me and France are
about to cease. But I shall always preserve the
memory of that adopted land. Assure the Emperor
of my good wishes. I hope that he will comprehend
my unhappy position. I will never consent to a
divorce; but I flatter myself that he will agree to
a friendly separation and will not conceive any resentment on that account. Such a separation has
become indispensable. It will not alter the sentiments of esteem and gratitude which I preserve."
Then she gave M. de Méneval a snuff-box, ornamented with her monogram in diamonds, and retired
to conceal her emotion, which was beginning to
overcome her self-control.

IX.

THE FIELD OF MAY.

ON arriving at Paris, M. de Méneval waited at once on Napoleon to give him the news so long expected with impatience. The Emperor was overwhelmed with sadness. On April 17, he had left the Tuileries, a dismal abode, full of gloomy souvenirs, and installed himself at the Élysée. There he could sometimes interrupt his immense labors by walks under beautiful trees, whose shadows cooled his fevered temples. He felt that, in spite of all his genius, the earth was failing beneath his feet. From afar he heard the tramp of innumerable battalions advancing upon France, and understood that, sooner or later, heroism must succumb to numbers. A profound melancholy took possession of his soul. He cast on men and things a glance that was discerning but discouraged. If his son had been there, if he could have rested his eyes upon the blond head of his sweet and amiable child, he might have had some moments of repose. But the King of Rome was far away. The prisoner of the Coalition, he had the destiny of Astyanax, — that fatal destiny which his father had foreboded.

138

M. de Méneval found the Emperor sitting on a tête-à-tête, his head resting on his hand, plunged apparently in a sombre reverie. Having received his faithful servant with great cordiality, Napoleon took him into the garden, where he plied him with questions. The least details about his son were in the highest degree interesting to his paternal heart. All that he said of the Empress was full of deference and consideration. He deplored the trials to which she had been exposed, and while recognizing that her sentiments toward France and himself had been violated, he was ready to go even further than M. de Méneval to find excuses for her.

When they came to political topics, the Emperor said that it was the Duke of Orleans, and not Louis XVIII., whom he had dethroned by returning from Elba, for the latter would not have been able to reign in France six months longer. He regretted it, because the Duke was the only Frenchman of his family. "Napoleon was touched by the patriotic sentiments displayed by the Duke of Orleans two months before, in going to assume command of the Army of the North, placed under the orders of Marshal Mortier; also with the letter he had written to this Marshal on returning in the retreat; and, above all, by the words reported by Captain Athelin, one of his aides-de-camp, whom the Duke of Orleans had authorized to resume his post as an orderly officer of the Emperor. The Prince said to him that the first thing necessary was to prevent another foreign invasion of France, and that he esteemed him fortunate in being able to resume colors which he had himself abandoned with regret."

Afterwards Napoleon spoke with tranquillity concerning the sovereigns, his pitiless enemies. What had occurred did not surprise him. He had comprehended, when attempting his enterprise, that he could count on nothing but the courage of the nation and his own sword. " For the rest," he said with a melancholy smile, " God is great and merciful."

After relating this conversation, pathetic in its simplicity, M. de Méneval adds: " All his language was marked by a calm sadness and resignation which made a vivid impression on me. I no longer found him animated by that certainty of success which had formerly rendered him so confident; it seemed as if that faith in Fortune which had emboldened him to form the hardy enterprise of coming back from Elba, and sustained in his march through France, had abandoned him at his entry into Paris. He felt that he was not seconded with the ardent and devoted zeal to which he had been accustomed, and that his movements, hampered by the trammels he had submitted to, had no longer the same freedom."

The unhappy Emperor could no longer entertain any illusions, either concerning the ingratitude of his wife, the hostility of his father-in-law, or the hatred of the kings who were once his vassals. Treated like a pariah by his enemies, he was put under the ban of Europe, and held up to public vengeance as the vilest of criminals. And yet he did not complain. His voice, once so haughty and so terrible, softened almost to prayer. He desired to be moderate, just, pacific. He invoked with sincerity those great moral laws which of old he had so frequently forgotten. Ah! if he could but apply his powerful intelligence to works of civilization, if he could be the benefactor of France and of Europe, if he could at last appear in the character of a gentle and beneficent monarch, could administer justice beneath an oak, like Saint Louis, and merit, like Louis XII., the name of the father of the people! But a mysterious voice said to him, "It is too late." Warlike in his own despite, he was condemned to war by fatality — and what a war! In meditating on the final struggle in which he was about to engage, he sometimes said that perhaps, like Louis XIV., he should gain a victory of Denain; for the next battle, the decisive battle, he would give himself, and, as a general, he certainly was not inferior to Villars. Alas! the France of 1815 did not resemble the France of 1712. That France was ruined, enfeebled, harassed, but it was united, and even the peasants who browsed on herbs like cattle, still cried, "Long live the King!" But this France, though less exhausted, lacked unity and concord. In Vendée there had been a rising against the tricolored flag. In every department of the Empire the Royalists made no secret of their desire for the foreigner's success. The saying of the Gospel was about to be realized, "Every house divided against itself shall perish."

One might have said that the same country contained two different nations. In spite of the absolute centralization which the Revolution thought it had established, there was no unity in France, and the two flags symbolized the bitter dissensions which divided its citizens from one another.

It was in vain that Napoleon made a loyal trial of liberty. Nobody believed in the sincerity of his intentions. The enemies of the Empire continued to repeat that the Additional Act was only a decoy. The journals used the freedom accorded to them merely to paralyze the national defence by their criticisms and their alarms. Napoleon recalled his brother Lucien, whom public opinion approved for having more than once refused a crown. The time was long past when it was an unpardonable crime for a brother of the new Charlemagne to have married a private person. Napoleon put around Lucien's neck the broad ribbon of the Legion of Honor which he had worn himself when coming from Elba to Paris. " It is too disgraceful to me that you should not have it," he said to him.

Lucien installed himself in the Palais Royal and made up his household. He retained in his service all the domestics of the Orleans family who were willing to remain. He found Napoleon sad and weary. " He has a great propensity to sleep," said Lucien; "it is an effect of his malady. He is surprised himself that, with this habitual drowsiness, he should have had the energy to return from Elba.

He is projecting a Field of May," adds Lucien, "where I proposed to him to abdicate. It seemed to me that he was not very unwilling. A few days later, instead of the abdication, he communicated to me his Additional Articles. I dared to contradict him. 'A million of souls missing at the least,' said I to him. He treated me like a driveller. He got into a rage, just as he used to. I bore it in silence; the situation is so different! Inwardly I said, 'Alas! he is unchanged.' He declared that he would not permit me to have a seat in the legislative body. He suspects me of a secret ambition to be elected president of it, with the idea of making a new 18th Brumaire against him. I was angry and went away. Joseph reconciled us. The costumes were decided on for the ceremony of the Field of May. I said I would not wear white, but simply the uniform of the National Guard. The Emperor said with a disagreeable smile, 'Yes; so that you as a National Guard may produce more effect than I as Emperor — is that it?' I decided to wear white."

While the preparations were in progress for the Field of May, Napoleon heard something which afflicted him all the more because he saw in it a sinister presage for himself. In vain had Murat, his sole ally, essayed to rouse Italy against Austria, and dreamed of the part which Victor Emmanuel played successfully later on. At Rimini, on March 31, he had issued this proclamation: "Italians, you were once masters of the world, and you have expiated your glory by twenty centuries of oppression. Make it to-day your ambition to have no more masters. Seas and inaccessible mountains, these are your boundaries. The question is whether Italy shall be free, or whether you will submit to foreign domination. I call to my side all the heroes of Italy." This first germ of Italian unity was stifled. The cries of "Long live Joachim the Italian!" remained almost unechoed. The daring sovereign was completely beaten at Tolentino by two Austrian generals, Bianchi and Neipperg — Neipperg, the man fatal to Napoleon. On May 19, Murat, a fugitive and obliged to hide himself, reached Naples in the night. "Madame," he said to his wife, when talking with her for the last time, "do not be surprised to see me living; I have done all that I could to die." Then he left Naples as he had entered it and took refuge at Ischia, whence a merchant vessel brought him to Toulon. A few hours later his wife negotiated the surrender of Naples with the English and the Austrians, and embarked for Trieste. On May 20, exactly two months to a day after the tricolored flag had been raised upon the dome of the Tuileries, the Bourbon standard was run up on the walls of the capitol of the Two Sicilies. Napoleon, dreading the contagion of misfortune, would not permit Murat to come to Paris. He exiled him to Provence. It seemed to him that his own fate was foreshadowed in that of his brother-in-law. One might call Tolentino the prologue of Waterloo. The vanquished, ill-

omened man was not to appear on the Field of May—
and yet he would be so useful to head the French cavalry at the time of the final struggle in which the
Emperor is preparing to engage!

The ceremony of the Field of May had at first
been intended to celebrate the inauguration of the
liberal Empire and the coronation of Marie Louise
and the King of Rome. But this second part of the
original programme had to be abandoned, since the
implacable Coalition had deprived Napoleon forever
of his wife and child. A proclamation of the votes
on the Additional Act, and a distribution of flags
was all that remained. The votes were as follows:
Affirmative, 1,300,000; negative, 4206. The affirmative votes for the Consulate for life had been
3,577,259, and for the institution of the Empire,
3,572,329. This diminution shows how much ground
the Empire had lost. As to the Chamber of Representatives, hardly one hundred thousand electors
made their appearance in the electoral colleges.
Real enthusiasm no longer reigned anywhere except
in the army, and it alone gave prestige to the last
fête of the Empire. As usual, the account of it in
the *Moniteur* was a dithyramb. "Never was there
a fête more national," said the official journal, "never
did a spectacle more imposing and more affecting
meet the eyes of the French people. All that takes
possession of and elevates the soul, the prayers of
religion, the pact of a great people with its monarch,
France represented by the élite of its citizens, culti-

vators, merchants, magistrates, warriors, assembled around the throne, an immense population covering the Champ-de-Mars and uniting itself in spirit to the great objects of this magnificent ceremony, excited as ardent enthusiasm as any of which the most memorable epochs have left a souvenir." A good deal must be subtracted from this lyricism. Sadness underlay all the solemnities, and sombre presentiments took possession of men's souls.

In the Champ-de-Mars, the theatre of the Federation of July 14, 1790, there had been erected in haste some decorations as ephemeral as everything else was in those days. The imperial throne was placed in front of the Military School, in the centre of a vast semicircular enclosure with double tiers of seats to right and left, forming an amphitheatre capable of seating fifteen thousand spectators. A third tier, facing the throne, was open, and an altar was set up in the middle of it. About six hundred feet beyond the altar rose another solitary throne which dominated the entire Champ-de-Mars. Troops to the number of fifty thousand, twenty-seven thousand of them being National Guards, passed in review before the Emperor. An immense crowd covered all the rising grounds of the Champ-de-Mars even to the Seine.

Napoleon made his appearance in the carriage used at his coronation, drawn by eight horses; he wore the silk habit, the plumed hat, and the imperial mantle. Nothing was lacking to his cortege, neither great officers of the crown, chamberlains, pages, nor heralds-at-arms. The marshals rode on horseback beside his carriage. His brothers, Lucien, Joseph, and Jerome, wore mantles of white taffeta embroidered with gold, and the Arch-Chancellor Cambacérès one of blue velvet sown with bees.

Let the Emperor enjoy for the last time the joys of sovereignty! Let him meditate on these theatrical pomps whose inanity he must by this time comprehend! These daises, this tinsel, these plumes, this gilding, — how much longer will they last? At the bottom of the censers but a few grains of incense now remain. What has become of the time when the great nation believed itself invincible? How different from the present solemnity was that of the distribution of the eagles on the morrow of the coronation! How sad they look, this King of Spain, this King of Westphalia, for whom so much blood has been shed in vain! And the Empress, the King of Rome, who were to be crowned on this Field of May, what has Providence done with them? There is no concord in the fête. The Royalists secretly desire the coming of the foreigners. The Republicans regret to see the Emperor displaying those pomps of monarchy which appear to them anachronistic. The sceptics make many reflections when they behold, on the steps of the throne, Carnot, once a member of the Committee of Public Safety, now a Count of the Empire; and beyond him Barrère, the Anacreon of the guillotine. The ceremonies, splendid as they are, are like the reproduction of an obsolete play. People scarcely listen to the Mass, which is said by the Archbishop of Tours, assisted by the Archbishop of Bourges and two other prelates. The official world turn their backs to the altar. The drums beat, and the Emperor rises to make his speech. Everybody pays attention; so many conjectures have been made concerning this discourse! Some imagine that he is about to announce the speedy arrival of his wife and son; others, that he will abdicate either in favor of the King of Rome, or to proclaim the Republic. Others still, and these are his most ardent partisans, think he is going to declare the country in danger, and name himself Dictator. All these previsions are incorrect. The Emperor announces nothing new in his discourse, and he ends it thus: "Frenchmen, my will is that of the people; my rights are theirs; my honor, my glory, my happiness, cannot be other than the honor, the glory, and the happiness of France." Then he swears allegiance to the Constitution, with his hand on the book of the Gospels, presented to him by the Archbishop of Bourges. Then rise shouts of "Long live the Emperor!" with which some cries of "Long live the Empress!" mingle, and awake at first a sentiment of surprise. Does Marie Louise merit to be thus acclaimed? But the soldiers, the heroic soldiers, still desire to believe in her; and after a moment's silence, the military deputations brandish their swords and cry: "Long live the Empress! Long live the King of Rome! We will fetch them hither!"

Then the Emperor descended from the throne, and throwing off his mantle, he places himself on the first step of the pyramidal platform which stands in the middle of the Champ-de-Mars. "Soldiers of the National Guard of the Empire," he says, "Soldiers of the army and navy, I confide to you the imperial eagle of the national colors. Swear to defend it with your blood against the enemies of the fatherland. Swear to die rather than suffer strangers to make laws for the fatherland." A formidable cry arises: "We swear it!" Deputations from the different departments commence filing past. To those from the Vosges, Napoleon says: "You are my old companions"; to those from the Rhine: "You have been the first, the most courageous, and the most unfortunate in our disasters"; to the departments of the Rhone: "I was brought up among you"; and to others: "Your phalanxes were at Rivoli, at Arcole, at Marengo, at Austerlitz." The ceremony becomes really grand, for the army has retained all its prestige. Here is the Imperial Guard marching by. "Soldiers of the Old Guard!" cries Napoleon, "swear to surpass yourselves in the coming campaign. Swear, all of you, to perish rather than suffer the foreigner to dictate laws to our country." In a time of apostasies and perjuries, these men will keep their oath. They will not conquer; they will die.

The solemnity is over. It has been more like a funeral than a fête. The bands have been as noisy as ever, but there has been nothing joyous in their music. The drums should have been muffled in crape. Every one feels vaguely that the duel in which France is about to engage with Europe is unequal, and that sooner or later it must succumb. Napoleon no longer places confidence in his star. He feels himself already condemned by fate, and the splendid display of the Field of May has not for an instant distracted him from his sombre thoughts.

Four days afterward, — Sunday, June 4, 1815, — the Emperor appeared at the Tuileries for the last time but one. Seated on his throne, he saw defile before him the electoral college, and deputations from the army and navy. Afterwards he assisted at Mass, and then went with his attendants to the great gallery of the Louvre, adorned with the masterpieces of painting, and there he conversed with everybody in an affable and easy way. At eight in the evening, a magnificent illumination irradiated the façade of the Tuileries. An immense crowd, returning from the Champs-Élysées, where public games had been going on all day, had stopped before the Pavilion of the Horloge to listen to a grand concert. At nine, Napoleon, surrounded by his household, came out on the balcony and gave the signal for the fireworks to be set off in the Place de la Concorde.

Bitter derision of Fortune! This fête preceded by only fifteen days the greatest disaster of our history. Ah! it was not illuminating lanterns which should have been lighted, but funeral torches; and since there was to be a concert at the Tuileries, they should

have chanted lamentations and canticles of death.
This throne, surrounded for the last time with so
much splendor, cracks already, and is about to fall to
pieces. One would say that France was singing to
deafen its own ears. As he looks down at the lights
with which the garden sparkles, the Emperor thinks
of the coming flashes of the bursting shells. Perhaps
a sinister vision rises before him. In a few days, the
Tuileries will be again illuminated, but this time it
will be to honor the re-entrance of Louis XVIII.
The gaiety of the people is forced. Doubt pierces
through enthusiasm, and though the *Moniteur* keeps
up its lyrical attitude as heretofore, yet *Mene, Mene,
Tekel, Upharsin*, flame on the palace walls. In returning to the Élysée, the Emperor asked himself this
question, full of anguish, "Will there be any more
fêtes for me at the Tuileries?" and a mysterious
voice answered, "No." Adieu majesty of the throne;
adieu great retinues; adieu resounding acclamations
of the crowd; adieu triumphant appearances on the
iron balcony of the Horloge Pavilion! Let the emperor give place now to the general, for war approaches
— war without its intoxications, without its trophies,
but with all it has of gloom, and anguish, and fatality; war with discouragement, panic, defeat, massacre,
and the order to retreat; war with all its horrors,
and not one of its dazzling illusions; war such as it
appears to philosophers by whom it is cursed, and to
mothers who detest it!

On June 7 took place the opening of the Chambers at the palace of the Legislative Body. Napoleon thus finished his discourse: "It is possible that the first duty of a prince may soon call me to lead the children of the nation in order to fight for the fatherland. The army and I will do our duty. As for you, peers and representatives, set the nation an example of confidence, energy, and patriotism; and, like the Senate of the great people of antiquity, resolve to die rather than survive the dishonor and degradation of France. The sacred cause of the fatherland will triumph."

No, the sacred cause of the fatherland will not triumph. For that, other dispositions would be necessary than those of the Assembly which, even while affecting devotion to the Emperor, was working clandestinely against him. During his speech some of the representatives seemed to be studying the efforts he was making to soften his voice, his gestures, and the expression of his face, and to assume the unaccustomed manners of a constitutional sovereign. Lafayette, who was vice-president of the Chamber, wrote to a relative: "You will be satisfied with Napoleon's speech; but I was not so with his face, which seemed to me like that of an old despot irritated by the part which his position forces him to play. Flaugergues and I were near him for a long time while people were getting into their carriages. 'You are looking younger,' he said to me; 'country air has done you good.' 'It has done me a great deal of good,' I answered. I could not return the compliment, for I found him greatly altered, and with a very extraordinary contraction of the muscles. As neither of us was willing to lower his eyes, each of us read the other's thoughts."

The address to the Chamber of Peers contained this remark: "If our success equals the justice of our cause, France cannot but reap peace. Our institutions guarantee to Europe that the French government cannot be carried away by the seductions of victory." And in his address to the Chamber of Representatives he said: "No ambitious design enters the thoughts of the French people; even the will of its victorious prince would be powerless to draw the nation beyond the limits of its own defence." Alas! these precautions against victory were most inopportune, most superfluous. Napoleon could not refrain from saying sadly to a deputation from the two Chambers when he appeared for the last time at the Tuileries, Sunday, June 11: "The struggle in which we are engaged is serious. The seduction of success is not the danger which threatens us to-day. The foreigners want to make us pass under the yoke of the Caudine Forks." And he ended thus his prophetic speech: "The Constitution is our rallying-point; it should be our polar star in these stormy moments. All political discussion which should tend to diminish, either directly or indirectly, the confidence people ought to place in its provisions would be a misfortune to the State. We should find ourselves in the midst of reefs without a compass and without a pilot. The crisis in which we are is very great. Let us not imitate the example of the Lower Empire, which, pressed on all sides by the barbarians, made itself a laughing stock to posterity by wrangling over abstract questions at the very moment when the battering-ram was breaking down the city walls."

On Monday, June 12, 1815, at half-past three in the morning, and after bidding adieu to his ministers and embracing Queen Hortense, Napoleon left the Tuileries to take command of the army which, six days later, was to fight at Waterloo. Catching sight of General Bertrand's wife just as he was about getting into his carriage, he took her hand, and said, as if he had already a presentiment of Saint Helena, "Let us hope, Madame Bertrand, that we may not soon have to regret the Island of Elba."

X.

WATERLOO.

"Waterloo! Waterloo! Waterloo! O plain of sorrow!
Like a wave that boils in an urn too narrow,
In thy circle of wood, and hill, and plain,
Pale Death commingled the ranks of slain.
There 'twas France against all Europe — impact gory!
There 'twas God betrayed the hero's hope of glory.
Thou hadst deserted, Victory, and Fate was worn.
O Waterloo! I weep, then cease to mourn;
For these last soldiers of our latest war
Were grand; the whole earth they had crushed before,
Chased twenty kings, crossed Alps and crossed the Rhine,
In brazen clarions sang their spirit fine!"

IT is thus that Victor Hugo, that Napoleon of poets, has had the force to celebrate Waterloo! But what a hymn of mourning! what a sombre and lugubrious harmony! Never has the French lyre given forth more doleful sounds.

Beranger, on his part, was unwilling that the fatal name of Waterloo should be pronounced in any song of his: —

"In Athens, who with Chæronea's name,
  Ever united sounds harmonious?
Dethroned by Fate, Athens cursed Philip's fame,
  And doubted gods once held victorious.

And such a day beheld our Empire fall,
  Beheld the stranger bringing in his chains,
Beheld even Frenchmen basely smile in thrall.
  Its name shall make no discord in my strains."

We find again the same sentiment which inspired the song-writer, at the close of the Memoirs of General de Ségur, who has traced the glories of the imperial epopee in prose, which at times assumes an epic turn. "Let others," he cries, "recite the heroic and marvellous details of Napoleon's return from Elba, his attempts, at first, to conciliate the Coalition, and then to prepare himself for the combat; in fine, his secret and sorrowful presentiments from the morrow of his arrival, his lost faith in his star, and the disastrous result of that third and last effort of an incomparable genius against his destiny, which had willed that the greatness of his elevation should equal that of his downfall. However worthy of memory on this subject may be the relations given me by eyewitnesses such as M. Mollien, my father, Benjamin Constant, Marshal Reille, Montyon, Turenne, Prince d'Eckmühl, and others, I own that courage fails me to recount so many bitterly painful details."

Alas! we cannot pass over this fatal day in silence. It is the denouement of the terrible drama whose vicissitudes we have essayed to trace. For a long time we hesitated; the pen dropped from our hand. This battle, more sombre than Cressy, or Poitiers, or Agincourt; this defeat, which has no more been avenged by France than Zama was by Carthage, this great national catastrophe, must be related.

Napoleon had only about one hundred and twenty thousand men to oppose to the two hundred and thirty thousand composing the armies of Wellington and Blücher. However, he did not despair of success, and he counted on renewing the tactics which had proved efficacious so many times already. To attack the two armies separately, to surprise the Prussians, and then to fall upon the English before they should have time to rally their different corps, — such was his plan of campaign. During the night of June 14–15 an ill-omened event occurred: General de Bourmont, followed by five officers, who, like himself, were Bourbon partisans, went over to the enemy. "Their names," the Emperor said, later on, "will be held in execration so long as the French people form a nation. This desertion increased the anxiety of the soldiers." On June 15, the French army crossed the Sambre, and, in a fiery proclamation, Napoleon reminded his troops that this day was the anniversary of Marengo and Friedland. A success of the advance guard encouraged them. The English were defending Quatre-Bras as a rallying-point, and the Prussians, Fleurus and Sombref. On June 16, while Marshal Ney failed at Quatre-Bras, the Emperor gained the sanguinary battle of Ligny against the Prussians. The struggle became ferocious by dint of being stubborn. It seemed as if each man recognized his mortal enemy, and rejoiced because the moment of ven-

geance had come. Quarter was neither asked nor
given. Blücher, who had had a horse killed under
him, in dismay ordered a retreat. But the untir-
ing septuagenarian's repulse had not been an utter
overthrow. The Prussians, who still numbered more
than ninety thousand combatants, retreated in good
order, and Marshal Grouchy, whom the Emperor
ordered to pursue them, had only thirty-two thousand. Napoleon turning back on the English army
at Quatre-Bras, Wellington evacuated the position
and retired to Mont-Saint-Jean, near Waterloo. The
forest of Soignes extends behind Mont-Saint-Jean.
The English general drew up against it. The hilly
character of the ground, which nature has fortified,
permitted him to maintain a formidable defence. The
troops on both sides were worn out with fatigue.
The temperature betokened a storm, and the air was
heavy, with thirty degrees of heat. In the afternoon
of June 17, the sky, which had been covered by thick
clouds, discharged them in torrents of water. At the
end of a few minutes the whole region was changed
into a hopeless marsh. The rain kept on all day,
all night, all the next morning. A solemn and terrible night was that of June 17–18, which has been
called "The Vigil of Waterloo." The two armies
face each other in that feverish expectation which
precedes decisive battles. No shelter against the
drenching rain. They stick fast in mud above their
knees. No moon, no stars. The darkness is profound, impenetrable. The men lose themselves in

quickset hedges. They stumble against each other and fall head over heels down ravines. Curses mingle with the roaring of the wind. The French army believed itself already betrayed.

What must be passing in Napoleon's heart? What is he going to risk, this great gamester, on his final throw? More than his life; his crown and his liberty: more than his crown and his liberty; the fortune of France. All these men who will see but one more sun, will die for him, for him alone. The horizon is all aflame with bivouac fires, as it was on the eve of Austerlitz. But they are not now omens of good fortune as they were in 1805. These lights resemble a conflagration more than an apotheosis. Napoleon does not sleep. He had been eighteen hours in the saddle on June 15, and had slept but three hours before the battle of Ligny. On the 16th, he was again for eighteen hours on horseback. On the 17th, he rose at five in the morning. On the night of the 17th and 18th, it is he who makes the reconnoissance, his feet in the mud, his head under the bridle-bits. In vain he seeks to remind himself of all his victories, to take his former attitudes, to make effective speeches as of old. At heart he is troubled. To his physical fatigue a moral one is added. Once too greedy of emotions, he is now sated with them. His officers, his soldiers, are not less perplexed than he is. Their devotion is boundless, but it assumes the character of rage, of frenzy. The chiefs feel themselves still more threatened by the balls of a French reaction than by those of foreigners. An indescribable moral malady torments these men of bronze. The night seems long to them. They are in haste to precipitate themselves, heads lowered, into the tempest of fire, to seek there a refuge against the torment of their thoughts. But all these anxieties, these sufferings, these agonies, seem to concentrate themselves in a single soul, the soul of Napoleon. His eagle eye measures the profundity of the abyss. He knows what his defeat will be if he is vanquished. And yet his countenance betrays no anxiety. He seeks to convey to the minds of others a confidence which he does not feel, and, as in all great critical moments, he affects serenity and imperturbable calm.

Day is about to break. A few rays of pallid sunlight light up the fatal plain. Battle must be given at once, before the Prussians have time to come up. But the ground is so wet that neither the artillery, nor even the cavalry, can take a step. They will wait; and this waiting will be the ruin of the French army, whose sole chance would be to crush the English before the Prussians come. Alas! how often are the desires of man imprudent! What Napoleon desires above all is that Wellington shall not beat a retreat. The unfortunate Emperor longs ardently for the battle, and the battle will be Waterloo.

The rain has ceased. In a few hours the ground will be practicable again. Napoleon still has illusions. Having seventy-two thousand men to oppose to seventy-six thousand seven hundred, he relies on his genius to conquer. He would have conquered, in fact, if he had been joined by Grouchy instead of being outflanked by Blücher. All depends on that. If the English and Prussians make their junction on the field, the French army will be destroyed. The Emperor will not even admit that such a contingency is possible. At half-past eight, when breakfasting, he says to the generals surrounding him, "There are ninety chances for us to ten against us."

The Imperial army moves forward in eleven columns, and descends from the high grounds it had occupied to take up its positions for fighting. These eleven columns, which an English historian has compared to enormous serpents, their scales shining in the sunlight, march slowly to the sound of trumpets and the beating of drums. The military bands play the *Chant du départ*, and the famous air, *Veillons au salut de l'Empire*. It is half-past ten. Napoleon passes in front of the troops, who are drunk with enthusiasm, and utter frenzied acclamations.

At half-past eleven, the Emperor gives the signal: the cannonading begins. The French take the wood of Goumont. The ground has dried up. It will be soaked again, not with water, but with blood.

A few leagues distant, near Ghent, a man who is taking a solitary walk through peaceful fields, and reading Cæsar's Commentaries as he goes, stops to listen to some vague, far-off rumbling noise. He asks himself whether it is not the rolling of distant thunder, and seeing that the sky is still full of clouds, he deliberates whether to continue his walk or return before the storm breaks. Again he listens. No more noise, unless it be the cry of a waterfowl in the rushes, or the striking of a village clock. He goes on his way. The rumbling recommences. Is it the sound of a battle? he asks himself. A south wind, rising, brings distinctly the distant echo of the detonation of artillery. Now no more doubt. It is a battle. What a striking contrast: here, calm unalterable; a few women weeding among the beans: down yonder the unchaining of a hell, the rain of fire, the hurricane of howitzers and shells.

This solitary stroller is a Frenchman, the bitter enemy of Napoleon, the author of the *brochure*, *Buonaparte et les Bourbons*,— Chateaubriand. "Silent auditor of the formidable decrees of the Fates," he says to us, "I would have been less moved had I been in the midst of the mêlée. The peril, the firing, the pressure of death, would have given me no time to meditate; but alone, under a tree in the fields of Ghent, as if I were the shepherd of the flocks browsing around me, the burden of my reflections overpowered me." And he adds these noble words in which the partisan is silenced by the patriot: "Although Napoleon's success would mean to me an eternal exile, my country at this moment seized possession of my heart. My wishes were all for the oppressor of France, if, in saving our honor he could wrest us from foreign domination. Would Wellington triumph? Then legitimacy would re-enter Paris behind these red uniforms which had just redyed their purple in French blood. As the chariots of its consecration, royalty should then have ambulance wagons filled with our mutilated grenadiers. What would a restoration be, accomplished under such auspices? I recount but a very small fraction of the ideas which tormented me. Every discharge of cannon gave me a shock and redoubled the beating of my heart."

At this same moment, Napoleon is experiencing a still more violent emotion. Looking constantly in the direction whence he hoped to see Grouchy coming, he sees on the horizon, near the chapel of Saint Lambert, something indeterminate and vague which excites first his curiosity and then his fear. "What do you see towards Saint Lambert?" he said to Marshal Soult. The Major-General answered: "I think I see five or six thousand men. It is probably one of Grouchy's detachments." All the glasses of the staff are at once levelled on this point. Some think they are not troops, but trees; some that they are columns in position; others that they are troops on the march. If so, is it Grouchy or Blücher? On the answer to this question will hang the fate of the day. At such a distance it is impossible to distinguish the French uniform from the Prussian, as both of them are blue.

Then the Emperor calls my grandfather, General Domon, formerly captain of Murat's Guards, and orders him to make a reconnoissance with his division of light artillery, accompanied by that of General Subervic. If the troops are French, he will join them; if they are Prussians, he will keep them back. At the same time — it is an hour past noon — Napoleon sends a despatch to Grouchy ordering him to come up. But will the order reach him in time? And where is Grouchy? No one knows. At the same moment Marshal Ney attacks La Haye Sainte in an attempt to pierce the English centre. A furious struggle ensues, but produces no result. At half-past two, both armies, as if by a tacit understanding, accord each other a momentary truce, like two athletes who take time to breathe. The first act of the battle is over. They are already a long way off from those ninety chances against ten of which the Emperor spoke this morning.

A terrible piece of news reaches Napoleon: General Domon sends word that there is no longer any room for doubt: the troops debouching in the direction of Saint Lambert are Prussians; and Grouchy, instead of marching to Waterloo, is going toward Wavres. Perhaps this would be the moment to hurl all the troops upon the English army, before the Prussians arrive. But the great gamester hesitates to risk his last stake. He would like to preserve that marvellous Imperial Guard which has been so faithful to him, which is his pride, his glory. The thought that this army of Waterloo is his only one, while the military resources of the Coalition are inexhaustible, paralyzes his audacity. With his last army destroyed, what will then be left him. And, even granting a victory over the English and Prussians, with what shall he resist the innumerable troops of Austria and Russia?

It is three o'clock. The second act of the battle commences. The Emperor sends a brigade of cuirassiers as a reinforcement to Marshal Ney, who is still making heroic efforts to penetrate the English centre. And behold, without orders, and carried away by an instinctive movement, as if by the attraction of I know not what irresistible magnet, the whole cuirassier corps follows this brigade. The chasseurs and lancers of the Guard move in the same direction. In vain the Emperor cries, "It is too soon." The cavalry once started, nothing can arrest its rush. It is a torrent which carries everything away. Then begins an epic struggle, unexampled perhaps in the military annals of any people, a formidable duel of cavalry against a whole army, infantry and artillery, aided, too, by cavalry equal in numbers to the assailants. The Duke of Wellington will say, some years later, "I have never seen anything more admirable in war than the ten or twelve reiterated charges of the French cuirassiers upon troops of all arms." Ney has never been more intrepid. It is a miracle that this hero of heroes still lives. "Be sure, my friend," he says to General Erlon, "that for you and me, if we do not die here under the English balls, nothing remains but to fall miserably under those of the émigrés." Wellington is not less heroic. His tenacity is unshakable. To an officer who asks for instructions in case he should be slain, he answers: " I have no instructions to give; there is only one thing to be done — to fight to the last man and the last moment."

It is five in the evening. In spite of its furious charges, in spite of its gigantic efforts, the French cavalry cannot accomplish the impossible. It demands the infantry of the Guard, it demands the Emperor. Napoleon still hesitates. Physical sufferings come to add to his perplexities. He can hardly sit upon his horse. Instead of multiplying himself, as he had been used to on battle-fields where his presence diffused emulation and enthusiasm, he remains motionless, suffering so much that he falls at times into a sort of lethargy. What a gradation in the sentiments, which ever since morning have taken possession of his soul! At first, confidence, illusion, the intoxication of battle; then, suddenly, doubt, fear, augmenting from hour to hour, from minute to minute, the face which grows troubled, which at one moment becomes paler than a corpse; then the frightful truth appearing in its full proportions, the last hope crumbling, then cataclysm, overthrow, annihilation.

Grouchy does not arrive. Is he guilty? No. His instructions were obscure. The officer sent to meet him did not join him soon enough. In marching toward Wavres, the unfortunate Marshal thought he was acting in accordance with the mind as well as with the formal orders of the Emperor. He may have been mistaken, but he was so in good faith; and history, if it is just, will incriminate his loyalty no more than his courage. His highest ambition would have been the fate of Desaix. But, alas! the star of Marengo no longer shone.

Ah! what tortures, what anguish in the heart of Napoleon, that Titan thunder-stricken! The fatal moment has come when he must throw his last card upon the gaming-table, the card which means despair. Sixty-five thousand Prussians inundate the battle-field. They come to act in concert with fifty-five thousand Anglo-Germans. There remain only fifty thousand Frenchmen able to combat these one hundred and twenty thousand enemies. The infantry of the Guard are going to charge. The last act of the battle opens.

" All, those of Friedland and those of Rivoli,
  Knowing that on this holiday they were about to die,
  Saluted their divinity, erect amid the storm,
  One cry, 'Long live the Emperor!' the last their pale lips form.
  Then, with the music on ahead, all passionless and slow,
  And smiling at the English guns black yawning there below,
  The Imperial Guard went forward into the furnace flame."

Calm, silent, not firing a single gun, they cross the plateau, and march against the English lines. They are wiped out by cannon and musketry: out of the two thousand nine hundred heroes who offered this supreme attack, hardly eight hundred are left standing. It is nearly eight o'clock. All is over. The Emperor has lost the battle.

> "They went, all armed, front high, grave, stoical.
> Not one shrank back. Sleep, dead heroical!
> Their waiting comrades, wavering in their place,
> Beheld the Old Guard perish. — Then, with face
> All pale and scared, Disaster raised her voice
> Despairing — giant she, with moments choice
> To fright battalions haughty, and to change
> Their flags to tatters — spectre made of smoke
> Who as she rises grows — Disaster broke
> On every soldier's gaze, to every man,
> Wringing her hands and crying, ' 'Scape who can!'" [1]

Marshal Ney, hatless, his sword broken in his hand, his clothes ragged with bullet-holes, — takes a handful of men with him, and flings himself once more into the mêlée. "Come on, my friends," he cries; "see how a marshal of France dies." Alas! the hero will not die upon the battle-field.

Napoleon, owning himself vanquished, has just given the signal to retreat. It was to render that possible, and to avert the utter extermination of what had been the French army, that the veterans of the Guard had given themselves to death like the Spartans at Thermopylæ. The four or five squares of this heroic infantry in the midst of one hundred and twenty thousand enemies, resemble, as the national historian has said, the summits of a rock which the furious ocean is covering with foam. The Guard dies, and does not surrender!

---

[1] Victor Hugo, *Les Châtiments.*

A patriotic painter, Hippolyte Bellangé, whose radiant canvas, *La Revue au Carrousel*, has so well represented the joyous and triumphant army, has depicted the death agony of the Imperial Guard in one of the most striking pictures that exist. This painting, lugubrious and doleful, makes one shudder. The sky is sombre, gloomy — one of Géricault's skies. Behind a rampart of English corpses, in red uniforms, three grenadiers of the Guard still stand erect. One of them is firing his last shot. Another, making a furious gesture, shakes his clinched hand at the enemy. The third lifts his arms to heaven and cries once more, "Long live the Emperor!" The pen would essay in vain to describe what there is of ferocious energy, grandiose wrath, and heroic despair in the haughty attitudes and contracted features of these three veterans, dying as they had lived. Ill, and already himself taken possession of by the shadows of death, Hippolyte Bellangé collected all his forces to create this canvas, the testament, as it were, of his talent, so military and so French.

Honor to the grenadiers of the Guard, to the soldiers, men of the people, who have pushed further back the boundaries of devotion, courage, and the spirit of sacrifice! Their blood will be fruitful. In the eyes of posterity they will have elevated a defeat to the level of the most famous victories. Like the martyrs of religion, these martyrs of glory will have triumphed even unto death. *Gloria victis!*

And Napoleon, where is he? The shadows of twilight have overspread the plain. He is no longer seen. Some say that he is wounded, others that he is slain. The soldiers, no longer feeling themselves protected by his genius, break their ranks. There are some who blow out their brains, unwilling to survive defeat. Later on he will say, "Waterloo! Waterloo! It is there I should have died." Like Ney, he has not succeeded in getting killed. Surrounded by a square of grenadiers of the Guard, under command of Major Martenot, he is marching pell-mell with a crowd of wounded in the midst of a handful of veterans who make a rampart for him of their bodies. A few days later Wellington will write: "I cannot express with what regret and sadness I look around me. The dear-bought glory which follows such actions does not console. . . . In truth, the losses I have experienced have so beaten and broken me down, that I have not courage to rejoice over the advantages we have obtained." If the victor speaks thus, what must the vanquished say, when the vanquished is Napoleon? To the joyous music played by the bands this morning must succeed the *De profundis*, the *Dies iræ*, the lamentations of Jeremiah. What reflections must not he who had been the victor of Austerlitz have made at this moment on the pitifulness of ambition, the caprices of fortune, the immense share which is left to chance in earthly things, on the slender thread on which hang the occurrences of this world! A secret voice, more eloquent than that of any of the sermonizers who have exhorted against pride, was whispering in the fugitive's soul. The saying of the Gospel verified itself, " For all they who take the sword shall perish by the sword." They say that the man of bronze wept. To deplore such a catastrophe, would an ocean of tears suffice?

XI

THE battle of Waterloo was fought on Sunday, June 18, 1815. On that day the Parisians were reading in the *Moniteur* the proclamation of June 14, in which the Emperor had said to his army: " Soldiers, to-day is the anniversary of Marengo and of Friedland, which twice decided the destiny of Europe. Then, as after Austerlitz and Wagram, we were too generous; we believed the protestations and oaths of the Princes whom we left on their thrones. To-day, however, having combined among themselves, they seek to attack the independence of France and her most sacred rights. They have begun the most unjust aggressions. Let us go to meet them! Neither they nor we are any longer the same men!"

On Monday, June 19, — O irony of fate! — a hundred discharges of cannon from the Invalides announced a victory to the Parisians, — alas! a victory already old, — that of Ligny. The same day the Ghent *Moniteur* published the following: " The 18th ended, in the happiest manner, for the Allies, the

172

sanguinary and bitterly contested struggle which had lasted since the 15th. Bonaparte's army, French in name only, since it is the terror and scourge of the country, has been vanquished and almost utterly destroyed."

The immediate consequences of the battle of Waterloo were no less disastrous than the battle itself. Even nightfall did not interrupt the carnage. While the English army, worn out with fatigue, betook themselves to rest, the Prussian cavalry pursued relentlessly the flying French troops. The rising of the moon facilitated this man-hunt. At Ligny the Imperial Guard had cried " No quarter ! " and now the same cry came back upon them like the penalty of retaliation. Cannons, military wagons, baggage, obstacles of all sorts, made their road difficult. The confusion, disorder, and terror were inexpressible. History offers few examples of such an overwhelming disaster. At Charleroy the Emperor left his brother Jerome, whose conduct at Waterloo had been heroic, in command of the remnants of the army, and posted to Paris, where he knew that the Royalists, believing his sword broken, would like to break also his crown and sceptre.

The joyful salvos of artillery, fired by the cannon of the Invalides on June 19, had not reassured the Parisian population. Vague presentiments oppressed all minds. Towards six in the evening of June 20, an aide-de-camp of Marshal Davout, Colonel Michel, who had been sent by him for tidings, and had been present at the end of the battle of Waterloo, arrived in Paris at full speed, and announced the disaster to the Marshal. " I would have you shot for bringing me such news if I did not know you," cried the defender of Hamburg, roughly. And the Colonel answered, " Please God you might have me shot, if that would alter the case."

In the morning of June 21, Napoleon re-entered the Élysée, whence he had departed on the 12th. How much had happened in those nine days! Ah! how much reason he had had for the fear he expressed to General Bertrand's wife, at the moment of departure, lest he might come to regret the Island of Elba. What a difference between the return from Waterloo and the return from Marengo, Austerlitz, Jena, and Wagram! When he stopped at the flight of steps leading to the Élysée, General Drouot, who had just left the carriage with him, could not refrain from exclaiming, "All is lost!" Napoleon answered quickly, " Except honor." It was the first time he had spoken since quitting Laon. Leaning on the arm of Caulaincourt, who had hastened to meet him, he slowly ascended the staircase. " I need two hours' rest," he said, " in order to be able to think of my affairs. I am stifling! a bath! let them bring me a bath!"

At the Palais-Bourbon, although the Chamber of Deputies did not begin its session until noon, the greater part of the members had been on hand since morning, to receive news and talk about the situa-

tion. Fouché had said of the Emperor, " This un-
bridled gamester no longer knows even how to win a
game ; and what is to be done now with a player
who can only lose ? " Napoleon was going to be
betrayed by men as he had been by fortune. The
consequences of Waterloo were to make it resemble
the battle of Zama, not that of Cannæ.

Here begins the death agony of the Empire. It
will not be less lamentable than the agony of Royalty. Napoleon, this genius so haughty, so resolute,
so pre-eminently the man of action, the former arbiter
of destiny, the Emperor of the eagle glance, the soul
of fire and the will of iron, is about to show himself
as undecided, as feeble, as timid, as the martyr-king.
M. Alfred Nettement has made the same remark in his
excellent *Histoire de la Restauration :* " Here is a
man," he says, " who had led the world by a glance, a
nod ; who had kneaded Europe with his hands ; before
whom France had slain itself for years. But, the circumstances changing, the talisman of victory having
been broken abroad by Providence in the hands of
the conqueror, and the force of opinion which had
rendered all things easy and possible altering toward
him at home, the same man is feebleness itself : he
can do nothing against any one, and everything can
be done against him. Fouché lords it over him ;
Manuel braves him ; Lafayette imperiously demands
his abdication ; the Chamber of the Hundred Days,
which certainly had nothing in common with the
Convention, threatens to depose him, and gives him

but an hour to make his abdication. Louis XVI. was not more helpless, more inert, more inactive against his enemies. Let no one answer that Louis XVI. had not lost the battle of Waterloo: he had lost the battle of the seventeenth century against the eighteenth, of the monarchy against revolution, of religion against unbelief."

What a lesson for human pride is this impotence of Napoleon! And how Providence makes us as it were touch with our hands the nothingness of those things which men proudly call genius and glory, and which count for so little before the decrees of the Eternal! The Emperor in the Élysée is not less humiliated than the King in the Temple, and he is more to be pitied; for, in his misfortune he does not look toward the Crucifix!

After taking a few moments of repose, Napoleon held a council on that very morning of June 21. "If the nation rises," said he, "the enemy will be destroyed. If, instead of such a rising and a resort to extraordinary measures, we begin disputing, all is lost. The enemy is in France; in order to save the country I need great powers — a temporary dictatorship. I could seize it in the interest of the country, but it will be more useful and more national to have it given me by the Chambers." Alas! the Emperor will not be treated by the Chambers as the Consul Varro was by the Roman Senate. Carnot alone supported the idea of a dictatorship. The former Conventionist bethought himself of the fourteen armies

of the French Republic. But he obtained no follow-
ers. The flame of 1792 was burnt out. Paris had
no desire to imitate Saragossa. The unfortunate
Emperor saw the traces of absolute discouragement
upon the faces of his ministers. Regnault de Saint-
Jean d'Angely, one of his most faithful adherents,
suggested, in respectful terms, an abdication in favor
of the King of Rome. But listen to Lucien Bonaparte, a member of the Council: "The assembly was
very disorderly. An abdication in favor of the King
of Rome was proposed as delicately as possible. —
'The Bourbons would be preferable to my son,' said
Napoleon; 'they are French, to say the least.' I am
not one of those who find this reply admirable," adds
Lucien. "At that moment nothing was more French
than his son."

But, no matter what Lucien may say, Napoleon
was not deceived. He knew that his son was the
prisoner of the Coalition, and that the Coalition would
not loose its prey. As to Marie Louise, he was only
too certain that he had nothing to expect from her.
"They tell you," he exclaimed, "that the King of
Rome, under the regency of his mother, would be
admissible. It is a perfidious fable, invented at
Vienna and circulated in Paris so as to bring about
our ruin. I know what is going on at Vienna, and
that my wife and son would not be accepted at any
price. They want the Bourbons and nothing but the
Bourbons, and it is entirely natural. When I am got
rid of, they will march on Paris, re-enter it, and pro-

claim the Bourbons. Do you want them? For my part, I don't know that they are not preferable to anything else I see." In vain the Emperor developed, in glowing terms, the resources he could still draw from the soil of France; in vain he described the prodigies which might be accomplished by union and perseverance. He convinced no one. They would decide on nothing. They would await events.

What was going on at the same time in the Chamber of Deputies? After a silence which had lasted twenty-three years, Lafayette, the friend of Washington, the leader of 1789, the prisoner of Olmutz, ascended the tribune. "When for the first time, after so many years," said he, "I lift a voice which the old friends of liberty will recognize again, I feel myself called to speak to you of the dangers of the country, which you alone have now the power to save. Sinister rumors have been circulated; unfortunately, they are confirmed. Now is the moment for us to rally around the old tricolored standard — that of '89, of liberty, equality, and public order. It is that alone which we have to defend against foreign pretensions and internal attempts. Permit, gentleman, a veteran of this sacred cause, who was always a stranger to party-spirit, to submit to you some preliminary resolutions whose necessity I hope you will approve."

Then he demanded that the Chamber should declare itself permanently constituted, and consider any attempt to dissolve it a crime of high treason; also, that the Ministers of War, the Interior, and Police should be requested to report at once to the Assembly.

" The anachronism of this discourse," Chateaubriand has said, " caused a momentary illusion. It seemed as though the Revolution, personified in Lafayette, had issued from the tomb and presented itself, pallid and wrinkled, on the platform." And yet this revolutionary motion, essentially unconstitutional because it deprived the sovereign of one of the chief prerogatives of the crown, the right of dissolution, was accepted without a contest by the Chamber, already faithless to the oaths taken but a few days before.

What will the Emperor do when he learns of this resolution which is equivalent to a deposition ? Napoleon wavers; his soul is troubled with uncertainties, fluctuations, contradictions. Now he is elated, now cast down ; to anger, recriminations, invectives, and menaces, succeeds silence ; to the over-excitement of a man who, remembering his glory, perhaps believes himself still capable of miracles, the anguish of a condemned wretch who feels the earth failing beneath his feet and sees the abyss open. He knows that if he gives orders they will not be obeyed. His voice, which once made the universe tremble, now intimidates no one. The giant of battles has become as inoffensive as a child. He has less influence than Fouché, the Conventionist, the regicide. He counts for nothing any more. He can hardly believe his eyes and ears.

At Elba he was still adored.   At the Élysée he is but a phantom.   He reminds one of Bossuet's sermon against ambition, a sermon which is like a prophecy: " Behold a man so fortunate that a century sees not many like him; and then behold his ruin and his fall.   Because he has risen up so arrogantly, and lifted his head even to the clouds, and because his heart is inflated with pride, for that reason, saith the Lord, I will cut him down by the roots; I will prostrate him with a great blow and level him to earth; he shall become a disgrace and be no longer able to sustain himself; he shall fall with a mighty overthrow.   All those who reposed beneath his shadow shall leave him in fear of being crushed beneath his ruins.   And yet they shall see him lying at full length upon the mountain, a useless burden to the earth."   Fatal hour for the conqueror!   It is himself who no longer believes in the first Napoleon — who does not even believe in the second Napoleon. It is for form's sake only that he consents to defend his son's cause.   He knows that it is as irrevocably lost as his own.   He smiles bitterly at the last illusions concerning the dynasty, still entertained by two or three faithful adherents, who are trying to cling to the floating wreckage of a sunken ship.   Death would be a refuge for him; but he had already tried to kill himself at Fontainebleau, in 1814, and without succeeding.   A second attempt at suicide would be only a clumsy imitation.   He must live to suffer, live to expiate.   His destiny weighs on him like a

cloak of lead. This man, once so full of his all-powerful personality, would like to flee from himself, to
lose, if possible, the consciousness of his identity.
He is about to let himself drift, like a drowning man
who, after having swum with all his might, and
reached the limit of his strength, contends no longer
with the waves, but abandons himself to them. The
athlete, once indefatigable, feels himself at last vanquished by that supreme power which atheists call
the force of things, and which the faithful call Providence.

His brother Lucien vainly counselled him to resist
the insolent resolution of the Chamber of Deputies.
The following dialogue took place between them : —

Lucien. "Where is your firmness ? Overcome this
irresolution. You know what it will cost you not to
dare."

Napoleon. "I have dared only too much."

"Too much or too little. Dare for the last time."

"An Eighteenth Brumaire ?"

"Not at all. A thoroughly constitutional decree.
The Constitution gives you that right."

"They will not respect the Constitution, and they
will oppose the decree."

"Better still ; in that case they are rebels, and you
dissolve them."

"The National Guard will come to their aid."

"The National Guard has only a resisting force ;
when it comes to action, the shopkeepers will think
of their wives and their shops."

"An Eighteenth Brumaire which should not succeed might lead to a Thirteenth Vendémiaire."

"You are deliberating when you ought to act.
They act and don't deliberate."

"What can they do? They are talkers."

"Opinion is on their side. They will pronounce
your deposition."

"My deposition? Would they dare?"

"They will dare everything if you dare nothing."

While the two brothers were talking thus, the
neighborhood of the Élysée was filling up with an
immense crowd of patriots, unwilling to despair, and
who, perceiving the Emperor, greeted him with frenzied acclamations. The Avenue Marigny was thronged
with common people and former soldiers, in whom
the national chord was vibrating. They implored
Napoleon to lead them against the enemy. They
received him with as much enthusiasm as in the days
of his greatest triumphs. And he, greatly moved,
could not refrain from saying: "What do these people owe me? I found them poor and have left them
so."

Away with you, ungrateful courtiers! Away, men
of the old régime whom Napoleon has endowed, en-
riched, overwhelmed with favors! Away, chamberlains who grimace and call your former master,
Buonaparte! It is in the cabins of the people that
patriotism and honor will take refuge.

The common people who have suffered so much
from Napoleon and for him; the poor women who

have given him the lives of their sons; the veterans
whose bodies are covered with wounds on his account;
the poor peasants who have been ruined by the invasion; yes, all those who have suffered, all who
have wept, not only pardon their Emperor, but still
console and glorify him in his misfortunes. The
nobles, on the other hand, with a few honorable ex-
ceptions, deny him even before the cock has crowed!

The shouts redoubled. "Well!" cried Lucien.
"Do you hear these people? It is the same thing
all over France. . . . Will you abandon them to factions?" Napoleon, pausing, replied by a gesture of
the hand to the enthusiasm of the crowd. "Am I
more than man," said he, "that I should be able to
bring back a thousand misguided deputies to the
unity which alone can save us? Or am I a miserable
partisan chief, willing to kindle unavailing civil war?
No; never. In Brumaire it was our duty to draw
the sword for the welfare of France; to-day we should
throw the sword away. Go and try to pacify the
Chambers; I can do everything with them; I could
do a great deal without them in my own behalf, but I
could not save the country. Go; but I forbid you,
above all, in going out, to harangue these people who
are asking me to arm them. I will attempt everything for France, but nothing for myself."

Lucien, in company with the Ministers, started for
the Chamber of Deputies, passing in silence through
the tumultuous sea of people. At the Palais Bourbon
he ascended the tribune. "Do not let us enter the trap

which the foreigners have spread for our credulity,"
he cried. "Their aim is to disunite us so as to conquer." He added that the French nation had always
been accused of lacking perseverance, and that the
moment had now arrived either to refute or to justify
this reproach; if they did not imitate the conduct of
Spain, Russia, and Germany toward their sovereigns,
history would rank them inferior to the Spaniards,
the Germans, and the Russians.

Lafayette, rising in his seat, replied: "The accusation just made is calumnious. By what right does
the last speaker dare to accuse the nation of levity,
and of lacking in perseverance toward the Emperor
Napoleon? It has followed him through the sands
of Egypt and the deserts of Russia; through fifty
battle-fields; in successes and in reverses, and it is
for having followed him that we have to regret the
blood of three millions of Frenchmen."

Manuel insisted on the necessity of distinguishing
the cause of the country from that of a man. Another
deputy, M. Jay, demanded an abdication. The Chamber nominated a committee to devise measures for
the public safety; in reality, to assume executive
powers. It was composed of five members: Lanjui-
nais, General Grenier, Lafayette, Flaugergues, and
Dupont de l'Eure, to whom five others, chosen by
the Chamber of Peers, were to be added. The
latter assembly selected three generals, — Andréossy,
Drouot, and Dejean; and two former Conventionists,
— Boissy-d'Anglas and Thibaudeau.

Lucien and the Ministers were no better received by the Chamber of Peers than they had been by the Chamber of Deputies. Everybody felt that an abdication, or, failing that, a deposition, was imminent. And yet it was but a few days since the Chamber of Peers had said in its address to Napoleon: "The interests of France are inseparable from yours. If success does not attend your efforts, reverses, Sire, will not lessen our constancy, and will redouble our attachment to you." And at the same time the Chamber of Deputies had said: "Resuming to-day the exercise of her rights, and rallying around the hero to whom she confides anew the government of the State, France cannot admit the distinctions by which the Allied Powers seek to veil their aggression. To attack the monarchy of its choice is to attack the independence of the nation." What did all these promises, all these fine speeches, amount to? They were empty phrases and nothing more.

Returning to the Élysée, Lucien bluntly told his brother that no alternative was possible except a *coup d'état* or an abdication. Napoleon hesitated. Silent and motionless, he was awaiting the decree of fate in a sort of torpor. During the night the Committee of Ten appointed by the two Chambers assembled. They decided to send to the camp of the Coalition a committee of negotiators, who should present themselves, not in the name of the Emperor, but in that of the Chambers. It amounted, in fact, to a deposition; it was the thing if not the word. Napoleon no longer either reigned or governed.

The next morning, Thursday, June 22, 1815, everybody waked with the instinctive conviction that the end was near. The agony was almost over; the death bell was about to toll. And still Napoleon had a faint glimmer of hope. He had learned that the troops under Marshal Grouchy, — thirty thousand men, — who were believed to have perished, were safe, and that the survivors of Waterloo were gathering at Laon. For a moment the man of battles thought of drawing his sword from its scabbard. It was too late. The Empire was to have its Tenth of August — and a Tenth of August when even its defenders would not fight.

The Chamber of Deputies had been in session since morning. Wavering and impatient, they complained because the unhappy Emperor had not yet signed his abdication. They were afraid of an Eighteenth Brumaire. The comparatively favorable news from the army disturbed instead of rejoicing them. They noisily demanded his abdication; they must absolutely have it at once, without any reservation or condition whatsoever. Lafayette instructed Regnault de Saint-Jean-d'Angély to go and tell Napoleon that he would be given an hour in which to abdicate, and that if he had not done so by that time, he would be deposed. The session was suspended. Even Lucien no longer counselled his brother to resist. It was finished. *Consummatum est.*

For a moment the man who was about to cease to be Emperor revolted against the insolent impatience

of the Chamber. "They want me to abdicate," he
exclaimed bitterly. "To-morrow there will be no
army. If they had rejected me when I landed at
Cannes, I could have understood it. To have thrown
me aside fifteen days ago might have been courage,
but to-day it is cowardice." For an instant the blood
rose to his face. "No," said he, "I will not abdicate.
The Chamber is composed of Jacobins, hot-headed
pretenders who want places and hope to profit by disorder. I ought to denounce them to the country and
turn them out neck and heels. The time lost may
be repaired." But this brief instant of anger and ex-
altation gave place to utter dejection. Napoleon
quieted down. The urgency of his advisers re
doubled: "It was never my intention to refuse to
abdicate," he said with a calm sadness. "I have been
a soldier, and I will again become one. But I want
to be let alone to think it over quietly in the interest
of France and of my son. Tell these gentlemen to
wait." Alas! this was the final throe of his agony.
The Chambers would not grant even another moment
to their sovereign. What torture! To abdicate like
this; to abdicate, not before a formidable Assembly
like the Convention, able to gather fourteen armies,
and make all the sovereigns tremble, but before a
mean and miserable Assembly, a moribund Assembly
which has itself but a few remaining hours of life!
And yet it must be done. Overpowered by destiny,
Napoleon bowed his head, and at the moment when
he took the pen with which he was to sign the fatal

act, he felt so discouraged that he did not even think of mentioning his son's name.

Listen to Lucien's revelations concerning this : "It was so little a question of his personal interest, and that of his family, that at first he dictated his abdication without speaking of his son; and when Carnot and I reminded him that, at least, he ought not to abdicate except in favor of Napoleon II., in order to eliminate the Bourbons, he replied, 'The Bourbons ! What of it ? At least they would not be under the Austrian ferule.' Such a sentiment from such a man needs no commentary; he smiled at the importance we attached to his appointing his son. 'The enemies are there,' said he, 'and the Bourbons with them. We must either repulse the first or submit to the second. United, we might still be able to save ourselves; divided, there is no resource except the Bourbons. As to me, my fate concerns nobody; I know adversity.' Nevertheless, we induced him to abdicate in his son's favor, but he did it without sharing our illusions, and as a thing of very slight importance."

The abdication so much desired by the Assembly, and which was to be its own abdication as well as that of Napoleon, was signed between midday and one o'clock. It is in these words: "Frenchmen, in beginning a war to uphold our national independ-ence, I counted on the union of all efforts and all wills, and on the support of all the national authori-ties. I was justified in hoping for success, and I

braved all the declarations of the Powers against me.
The circumstances appear to me to have changed. I
offer myself in sacrifice to the hatred of the enemies
of France. May it be that their declarations are sincere, and that they bear ill will to me only ! My
political life is ended, and I proclaim my son, under
the title of Napoleon II., Emperor of the French.
The Ministers will form provisionally the Council of
the Government. The interest I take in my son
obliges me to request the Chambers to pass at once a
law organizing the Regency. Let all unite for the
public safety and in order to remain an independent
nation. June 22. [Signed] NAPOLEON."

It was nearly one o'clock when the abdication was
carried by Carnot to the Chamber of Peers, and by
Fouché to the Chamber of Deputies. In this latter
Assembly, the reading of this act, so impatiently
desired, moved even the Emperor's enemies. The
Chamber decided that "a deputation, composed of its
president and other officers, should wait on Napoleon
Bonaparte, and express to him the gratitude and
respect with which they accept the noble sacrifice he
has made to the independence and happiness of the
French people." It is easy to understand what the
Emperor must have suffered in receiving this deputation, whose action resembled irony more than deference. In his Memoirs, Lafayette, while rendering
homage to the dignified attitude of Napoleon, insists
on the so-called majesty of this deputation of which
he was a member: "It was an imposing spectacle,"

he says, " this arrival of nine representatives of the
people, strong in the respect due to a National
Assembly, and coming to announce to him, who,
after having mastered all the sovereigns of the continent, still commanded the French army, his Guard,
and a great party in the faubourgs, that he was no
longer Emperor, and that the nation resumed the
government."

A legitimist historian has laid stress upon the pue-
rility of this unseasonable outburst of parliamentary
pride: " Human vanity, even in noble hearts," says
M. Alfred Nettement, " is subject to strange illusions.
Otherwise, General Lafayette would have comprehended that these nine representatives of an Assembly full of the remnants of '93, elected by several
millions of voters formerly picked out by Napoleon,
and this time inspired by Fouché whose influence
had been supreme in the half-deserted electoral colleges, represented nothing but that Assembly, its
petty passions, pretensions, and vanities, and cut a
very poor figure before this Emperor who had abandoned himself after having been abandoned by fortune. . . . It is difficulty, it is danger, which make
an action grand, and in the action just performed by
the Chamber there was neither difficulty nor danger."

Napoleon received the deputation from the Assembly with calm and dignified indifference. " I thank
you," said he ; " I desire that my abdication may
assure the welfare of France, but I do not hope it."
He terminated thus his brief allocution: " There is

no question of me, but only of my son and France. Believe me, be united." Then he bowed to the members of the deputation, who retired in profound emotion. Shortly after their departure he learned that the Chamber of Representatives, instead of proclaiming Napoleon II. and instituting the Regency, had appointed an executive committee without saying a word about the Empire and imperial institutions. Then he exclaimed: "I did not abdicate in favor of a new Directory; I abdicated in favor of my son; if they do not proclaim him, my abdication is null and void. It is not by crawling on the ground before the Allies that the Chambers can force them to recognize the national independence."

Meantime, scenes really tragical were passing in the Chamber of Peers. The man who uttered the most gloomy, most despairing words was the incomparable hero of the retreat from Russia, Marshal Ney, who, only four days before, had fought like a lion at Waterloo. Carnot had just read from the tribune a report exaggerating the military resources yet remaining to France. Ney arose. "The report is false," he cried; "false in every way. Grouchy cannot at most have more than twenty-five thousand men under his command. There is no longer a soldier of the Guard to rally: I commanded them; I saw them all massacred before I left the field of battle. The enemy is at Nivelle with eighty thousand men; they can reach Paris in six days: there is no way to save the country except by opening negotiations. I owe the

truth to my country. I am not one of those who consult their private interest alone. What can I gain
by the return of Louis XVIII.? To be shot." Alas!
this hero of heroes knew not how truly he spoke.

Lucien ascended the tribune. Treating a popular
monarchy just as if it were a monarchy by divine
right, he recalled the ancient formula, "The King
is dead. Live the King!" "The Emperor abdicates. Live the Emperor!" he cried. But his voice
found little or no echo. He took his oath to Napoleon II. No one imitated his example. Later, he
avowed himself that the imperial cause was lost.
"At the time," he writes, "the abdication seemed
disastrous to me, and I used all my feeble efforts to
avert it; I thought and said then what many Frenchmen still think and say; to me, at least, it appeared
an act of weakness. But now, being calmer, and
having long and thoroughly studied the man and
the act, I have greatly changed my opinion. . . .
That which was honorable, chivalrous, royal, for
Louis XVIII., would have been cruel, infamous,
sacrilegious for Napoleon; he was bound to abdicate
the throne by the very sentiment which made him
accept it. He would have been culpable if, for the
sake of defending his throne or that of his son, he
had braved civil war; and since, rightly or wrongly,
he did not think himself able to save France without
the Chambers, it was his duty to yield to the Chambers which, by a word, he could have overthrown."

General Labédoyère, however, seeing that the

rights of Napoleon II. were not recognized, cried
out in violent anger: "I heard voices salute the
successful sovereign; but now when he is in trouble
they are far away. There are some who are unwilling to recognize Napoleon II. because they want to
submit to the rule of foreigners to whom they give
the name of Allies. Napoleon's abdication is indivisible. If his son is not recognized, he should grasp
the sword, surrounded by Frenchmen who have shed
their blood for him and who are still covered with
wounds. He will be abandoned by certain vile generals who have already betrayed him. But if it is
proclaimed that every Frenchman who deserts his
flag shall be covered with infamy, his house torn
down, and his family proscribed, there will be no
more traitors, no more of the manœuvres which
caused the last catastrophe, and some of whose au-
thors are probably sitting here." At these inflamed
words the Peers grew pale with rage. "Order!
order!" was shouted on all sides. "Young man,
you forget yourself," said Marshal Masséna. "You
think you are still in the guard-house," said Lameth.

In all this there is, as Chateaubriand has remarked,
a nameless something which recalls those terrible
revolutionary scenes during the great days of our
adversities, when the poniard went round the tribunal in the hands of the victims. He writes:
"Some warriors whose fatal fascination has brought
on the ruin of France by determining the second foreign invasion, were disputing together on the thresh-

old of the palace. Their prophetic despair, their gestures, their words from beyond the tomb, seemed to announce a triple death, — death to themselves, death to the man whom they had blessed, death to the race they had proscribed."

Nothing will discourage the legionaries of the vanquished, dethroned, and imprisoned Cæsar. The white flag will reappear, but the common soldiers will hide their bitterness and their hopes beneath their thatched roofs, and proud of their glorious wounds, will recite to listening peasants the exploits of the tricolor. In the evenings they will sing the refrain of the popular song, " The Old Flag " : —

> " Here 'tis hidden 'neath the straw,
>   Flag that flew from field to field,
>   Sure to conquer, not to yield.
> Twenty years all Europe saw
> How it floated gloriously,
>   Crowned with laurels and with flowers.
>   When will come the happy hours
> When from dust I shake it free?

> " For a moment cast off fears —
>   Here, beside my arms it lies;
>   Come, my flag, my hope, my prize!
> 'Tis for thee to dry my tears.
> When the warrior's tears they see,
>   They will list, the heavenly Pow'rs:
>   Yes, they'll come, the happy hours,
>   When from dust I'll shake thee free!"

The 22d of June passed without Napoleon II. having been proclaimed. Instead of a regency, the

Chambers invested a committee of five of its members with sovereign powers.

The Bonapartists, however, were to make one last effort in favor of Napoleon II. This four-year-old child, the prisoner of Austria, was proclaimed Emperor of the French on Friday, June 23, 1815. But what a derisory proclamation! It was not the Chamber of Peers, every member of which had been appointed by Napoleon and overwhelmed by his benefits, but the Chamber of Representatives that set up this empire of a day, this purely nominal empire.

"Have we not a constitutional monarchy?" exclaimed Boulay de la Meurthe. "The Emperor dead, the Emperor lives. Napoleon I. has sent us his abdication, and we have accepted it. By that fact alone, by the force of things, by an inevitable consequence, Napoleon II. is Emperor of the French. You cannot even deliberate about the matter. Our fundamental law decides the question. . . . The Emperor's abdication is indivisible. . . . We are surrounded by intriguers and factious partisans who would like to have the throne declared vacant. . . . I will go further still; I will put my finger on the plague spot. There is an Orleans faction. It is useless to interrupt me. My information is explicit. I know that this faction is altogether Royalist. I know that its secret aim is to keep informed with regard to the patriots. However, it is not certain that the Duke of Orleans would accept the crown; but, if he did, it would doubtless be in order to relinquish it to Louis XVIII."

The Assembly was wavering and undecided. Being neither Republican, Royalist, nor Imperialist, it vaguely felt the falsity of its position. Manuel extricated it from this embarrassment by a speech which showed rare address. He proclaimed Napoleon II., but in a way which left a door of escape open to all parties. His harangue would not have been so cordially applauded had it been a real declaration of principles instead of a mere expedient. He began by saying that, "in proposing to proclaim Napoleon II. an inopportune and imprudent question was raised; but, since it has been brought up, to evade it would be impossible. The constitutional right being incontestable it must be affirmed." But how? Will the name of Marie Louise be pronounced? Will they establish a regency? By no means. The order of the day which Manuel succeeded in getting passed, alleges: First, that "Napoleon II. became Emperor by the fact of the abdication of Napoleon I., and in virtue of the Constitutions of the Empire"; second, that "the two Chambers, in naming a governmental committee, willed and intended to assure the nation of the needed guaranties for its liberty and repose in the present extraordinary circumstances." The nominal sovereign was to be Napoleon II., but the real sovereign would be Fouché, the President of the Executive Commission. But the Assembly appeared to take its vote as serious, and, as if wishing to put itself on good terms with its conscience, broke up with hypocritical cries of "Long live the Emperor!"

The reign of Napoleon II. was to be only a phantom, a vanishing dream. His Empire was no more real than his Kingdom of Rome. His two sceptres were broken like rattles, one after another. But will not his mother, at least, speak for him? It does not even occur to her to do so. The forgetful and unfaithful wife would not consent to leave her gilded prison, even though her jailers should open the doors. She does not wish her child to be anything but an Austrian prince. Nothing will remain of this title of Napoleon II. but the vote of an inconsistent Assembly and the immortal ode of a poet.

On that very evening of June 23, Fouché said to his intimates: "Everything is all right; we have confronted the old régime with the Constitutions of the Empire. I hope to see both pleaders back to back before long." And the next day he had the nominal accession of Napoleon II. placed on the minutes, but in his proclamation of the Provisional Government, he announced that all public acts would be performed solely in the name of the French people. He who had been Emperor two days before wanted to protest against this anomaly, but found no one willing to carry his protest to the Chamber.

The news of the abdication reached **Laon**, where the survivors of the army were assembled, on June 24, and caused inexpressible wrath and indignation. "Why should we fight any longer," said the soldiers, "since there is no longer an Emperor?" These indefatigable heroes, who did not despair of avenging Waterloo, declared themselves betrayed, and yielded to a very delirium of sorrow. At Paris, the old soldiers, the federates, the patriots who crowded the Avenue Marigny, were animated by the same sentiments. Fouché's government began to be afraid. It could not be easy while Napoleon was there; and in case he had not consented to go, they would probably have forced him. Marshal Davoust was sent to the Élysée to urge his old master to depart. Napoleon did not resist; he left Paris the next day.

At noon on Sunday, June 25, 1815, — the battle of Waterloo had been fought just a week before, — Napoleon left the Élysée Palace in a simple carriage and went to Malmaison. He drove through the avenue where, as if by a sarcasm of destiny, rose the colossal foundations of what was to be the Arc de Triomphe de l'Étoile. This avenue, once for him the route of ovations and of triumphs, must have occasioned him some bitter thoughts. It must have recalled the radiant morning of April 2, 1810, that day of incomparable splendor when he made his solemn entry into Paris with the young Empress Marie Louise. Where is that departed magnificence? The halt before the gorgeous decoration which simulated the present Arch of Triumph; the carriage drawn by eight horses, its gilded roof supported by four eagles with outspread wings; the Marshals of France on horseback at the sides of the imperial carriage; the applause of the crowd; the ringing of bells; the salvos

of artillery, the beating of drums, the blare of the
trumpets, — what is left of all that glorious pomp?
And the woman whom a delirious people saluted
with joyous homage; the woman to whom young girls
dressed in white offered gifts and flowers; the woman
whose arrival seemed the pledge of perpetual prosperity and peace; the young Empress of the French,
where is she at this hour when her husband begins
the stations of his Calvary? She is in the midst
of the enemies of France; she watches, unmoved,
the outbursts of their joy. It is even on this very
day, June 25, 1815, that at Baden, near Schoenbrunn, where she is occupying the same house with
her step-mother, Napoleon's bitter enemy, she learns
the tidings of Waterloo. Under the windows of this
house, common to both sovereigns, bands are playing
serenades to celebrate the victory of the Coalition.
What a Shakespearean contrast! On the same day,
Napoleon deposed, quitting his capital never to return; Napoleon proscribed, drinking to the dregs the
cup of bitterness as General and as Emperor, as husband and as father; and the Austrian musicians
playing triumphant music under the windows of
Marie Louise! Have the trumpets of Fortinbras at
the denouement of Hamlet a stranger sound?

XII.

MALMAISON.

THE most picturesque of historians, — he who has adopted as his programme that magical saying, " History is the resurrection of the dead," — Michelet, has said in one of his lectures: " Gentlemen, the greatest man of the world was a man. Now, he had a wife, and one day he wanted to change her for another. Great anguish, tears, lamentations. He said, 'It is only a woman!' You were not living during the Empire, gentlemen, but I was. I was a child then. I tell you, it was a time when nobody talked. The Emperor had done everything, you know; he had changed Europe and suppressed nations, and thrown the Republic out of the window. Nobody said a word; profound silence. One morning he wanted to send away his wife; all the world talked. Discussions began in every family. I heard this dispute between a man and his wife. The man said: 'She has given him no children. She has committed more than one fault. He might have divorced her when he came back from Egypt.' 'But he didn't,' said the woman. 'Why not now, then? The Emperor is all alone. Ought he not to surround himself with powerful families? His isolation is also that of France.' To which the woman, without arguing, simply answered: 'No matter; it won't bring him good luck.' 'And why not?' '*It won't bring him good luck!*'"

On that Sunday of June 25, 1815, when the vanquished of Waterloo found himself once more at Malmaison, that poetic residence, all filled with souvenirs of Josephine, in the depths of his soul he compared his second wife to his first one, and recognized — too late, alas! — how fatal to him the divorce had been. Evidently, feminine sentiment and popular instinct were not at fault: *It had not brought him good luck.* In re-entering Malmaison he forgot everything but Josephine: Josephine, whose sad and graceful phantom appeared to him in each apartment of the castle, and at the turn of every garden-path. Madame Caffarelli, an eyewitness, says that "he made no allusion to his situation, but talked about the domestic scenes in which he had participated here. At every door, at every window, he recalled either some remark of Josephine's, some jest of bygone days, or some amusement of their domestic life." Concerning the present and the future he said not a word. But the entire past revived again.

When the Emperor arrived at Malmaison, no one had dared to ask him any questions about his destination. They had left him to his reveries. It was a brief moment of repose on this Calvary whose stations might be called Malmaison, Rochefort, the *Bel-lerophon*, the *Northumberland*, Saint Helena. Napoleon reflected on worldly things as if they concerned him no longer. The inactivity of this man, once so pre-eminently active, had something terrifying in it. The next day, Monday, June 26, 1815, those about him broke the silence, and discussed before him the part he ought to take. The Duke of Bassano assured him that the people and the army were on his side, and that, if he chose, he could seize anew the reins of government, make himself obeyed by the troops, and dissolve the Chambers. When the Duke had gone out, Napoleon said with a melancholy smile, " Maret is always just the same, always ready to flatter me and himself, always ready to see and believe whatever he pleases."

On that day the Countess de Las Cases went to Malmaison to meet her husband. " ' My dear,' he said to her, ' in doing my duty I have the consolation of not compromising your interests. If Napoleon II. is to rule us, I am leaving you great claims upon him. If Heaven ordains otherwise, I shall have secured for you a glorious refuge and a name worthy of esteem. In any case, we shall meet again, even if it is only in a better world.' After tears and even reproaches, which could not but be sweet to me," goes on the author of the Memoirs, " she yielded and promised to rejoin me soon ; and from that moment I found nothing in her but elevated enthusiasm, and the courage which might have failed me if I had needed it."

The day passed, however, without the Emperor's having spoken of the future. He listened to all, and made remarks on what was said, but he manifested no resolve.

Tuesday, June 27. What is to become of the great Emperor, the proscribed man? Where shall he go? To America or to England? Will he be free? Will he be a prisoner? If he leaves Malmaison, this asylum of a few hours, who will protect him against such outrages as those which overwhelmed him a year ago, on his way to Elba? Is he not in danger of becoming a trophy of Blücher, or of falling under the blows of Royalist assassins? If he wishes to go to America, how is he to get to a port of embarkation? And, once at sea, how can he escape the English cruisers? Every one about Napoleon is asking such questions, but he himself seems to dread approaching them. In the midst of his distress there still remains I know not what vague hope of regaining his position. He expects unconsciously some miraculous event. He delays his departure from Malmaison as, in 1812, he delayed it from the Kremlin. One might say that a secret force retained him in this residence of his happy days, this gracious temple of his youth and glory. But time presses. The Prussians are coming. Whether he will or no, he must depart.

On the preceding day, June 26, the Provisional Government had issued a decree thus worded: —

" Article 1. The Minister of the Navy shall give orders that two frigates of the port of Rochefort be armed for the transportation of Napoleon Bonaparte to the United States.

"Art. 2. He shall be provided to the place of embarkation, if he desires it, with a sufficient escort, under command of General Beker, who is charged to provide for his safety.

"Art. 3. The Postmaster-General, on his part, shall give orders relative to the necessary changes of horses.

"Art. 4. The Minister of the Navy shall issue the necessary orders to assure the immediate return of the frigates after disembarkation.

"Art. 5. The frigates shall not leave the roadstead of Rochefort until the requisite passports have arrived."

It is from England, from Wellington, that the Provisional Government pretends to obtain these passports ; Wellington will refuse to give them. From hour to hour the situation becomes more difficult.

Presently General Beker, a member of the Chamber of Deputies, arrives at Malmaison. He comes to announce to the Emperor that he has been sent by the Minister of War to take command of the troops committed to him and to be responsible for the Emperor's person to the Provisional Government. At Malmaison there is a battalion of infantry and a hundred dragoons of the Imperial Guard.

While General Beker is taking command and being acknowledged by the officers, Napoleon, walking in the garden with the Duke of Rovigo, says to him :

" This smacks of a revolutionary committee rather than a generous government. I do not understand why the Minister of War did not communicate with me. Perhaps he saw nothing wrong in that, but at all events, the choice of Beker reassures me. Sieyès was right in saying they would abandon me. Still, I cannot go without vessels and passports; otherwise, the first village mayor could arrest me. All that would be necessary would be to tell him that I am carrying off treasure; he would write to Paris, the Provisional Government would not answer, matters would be precipitated, and that is how one would come to ruin."

General Beker was neither a jailer nor a traitor. He was an honorable man, a brave soldier, and the brother-in-law of General Desaix. According to Count de Las Cases, " Fouché knew that Beker had personal reasons to complain of the Emperor, and he expected to find him bitter and disposed to vengeance ; he could not have deceived himself more grossly. This General constantly displayed a respect and devotion most honorable to his character." Of tried loyalty, he was incapable of remembering that he had been disgraced in 1809. When he saw the emotion depicted on the General's strong countenance, Napoleon recognized at once that he had to do with a man of feeling. He gave him a friendly reception. To the very end he found in him a respectful servant and a friend in misfortune. But he distrusted the Provisional Government as thoroughly as he confided in General Beker. "Would they be capable," he asked, "of leaving me no alternative except that of giving myself up to my enemies?"

The same day the Minister of the Navy, Duke Decrès, arrived at Malmaison and communicated to Napoleon the following despatch from Fouché: —

"Paris, June 27, morning. To the Minister of the Navy. M. le Duc, it is urgent that the Emperor should depart. The enemy is advancing, and may be already at Compiègne. The Committee desire that you should repair at once to Malmaison to induce the Emperor to leave, because we cannot be responsible for what may happen. As to that provision of Article 5, of yesterday's decree, which relates to the passports, the Committee authorize you to consider it null and void. All the other provisions remain in force.

"[Signed]   THE DUKE OF OTRANTO.

"P.S. It is important that the Emperor should go in disguise."

The Minister of the Navy had hardly left Malmaison when the Emperor was informed of new contradictory instructions from Fouché, in which he said: "According to the despatches just received, the Emperor cannot leave our ports without safe-conducts. He must await them on the road. Consequently, the decree of yesterday remains in full force, and the letter written this morning to annul Article 5, is superseded. Guide yourself by the text of yesterday's decree."

It is impossible to mistake the intent of all these incertitudes and contradictory measures. As Walter Scott has said: "The members of the Provisional Government, like skilful fishermen, had gradually cast their nets about Napoleon, and they thought it was time to draw him to land." Let us render Duke Decrès the justice to admit that he made every effort to save the Emperor from captivity. The day before, June 26, he had written to him: "You will notice, Sire, on the list of American vessels, one which is now at Havre. The captain is in my ante-chamber. His post-chaise is at the door. I answer for him. To-morrow you will be out of reach of your enemies." Napoleon had refused this offer. To save himself clandestinely on a merchant vessel seemed to him unworthy of his glory; and when he saw around him a handful of young military heroes still dreaming of battles and adventures, and believing even at this moment in the possibility of avenging Waterloo, he did not wholly despair of drawing the sword once more.

Wednesday, June 28. The situation, however, was becoming more and more disquieting. It was to be feared, from hour to hour, that Malmaison might be seized by the enemy. Their cannon could be heard already on the plain of Saint-Denis: it was the second time in fifteen months that this disastrous sound had stupefied and afflicted patriotic souls. The bridges of Neuilly, Saint-Cloud, and Sèvres had been barricaded, and those of Saint-Denis, Bezons, Chatou, and Pecq destroyed. But these precautions could not protect Malmaison from a surprise. The Prussian fires could be seen on the other side of the Seine. The little garrison, comprising a battalion of infantry and a hundred dragoons of the Guard, under Generals de Flahault, Gourgaud, de Labédoyère, Bertrand, and Savary, made preparations for a vigorous resistance. Near the Emperor, however, all remained calm, and no one knew what decision he had reached when he summoned all his friends. " I have done all that you wished," said he. " Here are my letters to the Provisional Government and my correspondence with the Minister of the Navy. The difficulties they have put in the way of giving me two armed frigates have delayed me until now. It is their fault that I did not go sooner, but I am about to go."

Yet, even while making these preparations for departure, Napoleon still preserved a lingering hope. As Walter Scott has expressed it, he listened to the cannonading in the distance as a war-horse listens to the sound of the trumpet. Some officers from the army arrived at Malmaison, their uniforms covered with blood and dust, and besought their General, their Emperor, to place himself once more at their head. They informed him that the enemy had committed the imprudence of advancing in two bodies of sixty thousand each, which left them so far apart that Blücher might be overpowered before Wellington could reach him. Grouchy, having dexterously escaped from pursuit, was coming with fresh troops in excellent order: his advance columns were already approaching Paris by all the eastern routes, and there would be sixty thousand men to engage the sixty thousand Prussians, and to turn afterwards against the English. Napoleon thanked the officers for their news, and during the night of June 28–29, he ruminated the project of resuming command of the troops.

Concerning this project Walter Scott has said: " At a moment when the capital was about to be surrounded anew by foreign armies, an honorable sentiment, united to political considerations, might have made Napoleon hope that the representatives, in order to make use of his extraordinary talents, and his influence over the troops and the federates, who alone could defend Paris, would be disposed to lay aside personal animosities and permit him to resume his sword for the protection of the capital. But discord had made too much progress in the interior." In the night of June 28–29, at the very moment when Napoleon was beginning to cherish a last hope, Duke Decrès and M. Boulay de la Meurthe came to Malmaison to notify him of the definitive instructions of the Provisional Government. They were in this wise : —

" Long delays having elapsed since passports were demanded for Napoleon, and the existing circumstances arousing fears for his personal safety, we have decided to regard Article 5 of our decree of

June 26, as null and void. Consequently, the frigates
are placed at Napoleon's disposal. No obstacle to his
departure now remains. The interests of the State,
as well as his own, demand imperiously that he shall
start at once after you have notified him of our determination."

The Emperor replied that he was ready to go, but
would first despatch a message to the Provisional
Government.

Thursday, June 29.   At daybreak, Napoleon ordered his saddle-horses to be got ready, put on his
uniform, and summoned General Beker. He said to
him, in very nearly these words, " The enemy has
just made a great blunder, — one that might easily
have been anticipated, for that matter, from the character of the two allied generals. They have advanced
in two masses of sixty thousand men each, which has
left so considerable a distance between them that one
could be overpowered before the other would have
time to come up. We have here a unique occasion,
arranged for us by Providence, which it would be
both guilty and foolish in us to neglect. You know,
General, that at present all is lost; there is no hope.
Very well! let them give me back the command of
the army, and I promise to conquer at its head. Go
and present my request to the Executive Committee.
Explain to them thoroughly that I do not dream of
resuming power; I want only to fight the enemy,
crush them before Paris, shelter you all by a victory,
and constrain the chiefs of the Coalition to desire

peace. That done, I will continue my route toward exile. . . . I give them my word of honor, my word as general, soldier, and citizen, not to keep command an hour after the certain and brilliant victory which I promise to gain, not for myself, but for France. . . . Go, General; I confide myself to you. Aid me in this, and you shall never leave me again."

General Beker started immediately to Paris with this message, of which these are the concluding words: "The hurried march of the enemies upon the capital leaves no room to doubt their bad faith. In these grave circumstances, gentlemen, I ask to serve France for the last time, and I swear to save it."

On arriving at the Tuileries, General Beker delivered Napoleon's message to the five members of the Provisional Government. "What do you think of that?" said Fouché to his colleagues. "I think he is laughing at us. Come! this is going too far!" Then, turning toward the General: "Why did you bring such a message as that? Don't you know the situation? For Napoleon to appear again in command of the army would be equivalent to another disaster, and the ruin of Paris. Let him leave at once, for they are demanding his person, and we cannot answer for his safety more than a few hours." The General was instructed to carry back to Malmaison this laconic response of the five members of the Provisional Government: "The duties of the Committee toward the country do not permit it to accept the proposition and the active assistance of the Emperor Napoleon."

General Beker returned in all haste to Malmaison. He found the Emperor in uniform, either believing or feigning to believe that he might have received a favorable reply from Fouché. After reading the missive of the Provisional Government, Napoleon contented himself with saying: " These men are incapable of energy. Since that is the case, let us go into exile." He had his horses unsaddled, and replaced his uniform by a citizen's dress. A young merchant came hurriedly to warn him that in the plain of Saint-Denis he had seen three corps of Prussian cavalry which were following the course of the Seine and seemed to be approaching Malmaison. The Emperor thanked him for the information, and ordered the carriages to be brought up. His suite was divided into two parts. The first was composed of several carriages intended to contain M. and Madame de Montholon and their child, M. de Las Cases, his son, and several orderlies. They were to gain the Orléans road, pass through Chateauroux, and reach Rochefort on a certain day. The other division comprised only a single light calash, which Napoleon, General Bertrand, and the Duke of Rovigo were to occupy. The Emperor's valet was on the coachman's seat. A courier went ahead to order the carriages at the different post-stations.

The carriages destined for the first division drew up in the principal courtyard, in front of the vestibule of the chateau, while the Emperor's calash waited for him in the small court separating the house from the kitchens. Napoleon went to it through the winding alleys of the garden. He said farewell to his mother, his brothers, and his faithful servants. Queen Hortense begged him to accept a diamond necklace, so that he might have resources at hand which it would be easy to conceal. He refused at first. Hortense insisted: she wept. He yielded, took the necklace, put it in his coat pocket, and gave a last glance at the trees which had sheltered beneath their foliage so many joys and so much glory. Then he quickly entered the carriage, and seeing him depart, all the spectators melted into tears.

XIII.

ROCHEFORT.

THE heat was stifling when the carriage containing the Emperor and Generals Bertrand, Beker,
and Savary quitted Malmaison. Napoleon did not
speak a word, and his companions, as melancholy as
himself, respected his silence. The carriage, which
resembled a funeral coach, went through the woods
of Butart to Rocquencourt, and without passing
through Versailles, which was on the left, it went by
Saint-Cyr to take the Chartres road. They reached
Rambouillet at nightfall. The Emperor slept at the
chateau. It was the last imperial residence in which
he lodged. The same thing had happened to Marie
Louise. She had stayed there with her son from
April 13 to April 23 the previous year. It was there
she became the prisoner of Austria; there she had an
interview with her father; from there she started for
Vienna. Rambouillet, therefore, afforded Napoleon
a subject for some bitter reflections. As sovereign,
as husband, and as father, he must have yielded to
sorrowful meditations.

Friday, June 30, 1815. At a very early hour the

carriage containing the Emperor and the three generals left the chateau of Rambouillet by the path conducting to the park gate, which opens on the Chartres road beyond the town.

At the Chateaudun station the post-mistress came with a frightened face to the carriage door to inquire if the travellers came from Paris, and if it were true that Napoleon had met with misfortune. Hardly had she asked the question when she recognized the Emperor. Without another word she lifted her eyes to heaven and went back weeping into her house.

The travellers went on by Vendôme to Tours, which they passed through by night. The carriage stopped on the Poitiers road, just after leaving the city. The Emperor wished to see the prefect, and Savary going to fetch him, he talked for a quarter of an hour with this official. Then he resumed his journey, preserving the strictest incognito.

Saturday, July 1. They passed through Poitiers in the daytime. The heat was excessive. They stopped for a short time at the post-house, which was outside the town, and took some brief repose without being recognized.

At Saint-Maixent they found a crowd assembled in the square in front of the town hall. The National Guard were on the alert since the troubles had begun again in La Vendée. They stopped the carriage and demanded passports. General Beker showed his, and also the orders of the Provisional Government. No mention was made of the Emperor, and he was not recognized. The General's firmness succeeded in overcoming all difficulties, and they were allowed to go on. At nightfall they reached Niort, where they remained nearly two days. Napoleon still entertained a vague hope that some unforeseen event might recall him, if not to the throne, at least to the command of the troops, and not having abandoned the thought of going back, he travelled with intentional slowness.

Sunday, July 2. The sentiments testified by the people of Niort fed the last illusions of the Emperor. There were troops in the town intended to repress the rising in La Vendée. They gave Napoleon a very warm reception. As soon as his arrival became known, soldiers, citizens, and people of the lower classes crowded under his windows, demanding to see him. He appeared, and was greeted with cheers. The prefect begged him to stay at the prefecture, and he accepted the invitation. The day passed in profound emotion, shared alike by him and the population.

Monday, July 3. General Beker, always respectful toward the Emperor, told him in the morning that it might be dangerous to delay in this manner, as there was reason to fear the arrival of an English fleet before Rochefort, which would render his departure for the United States impossible. Napoleon allowed himself to be convinced, and left Niort, but not without regret. A detachment of light cavalry escorted him. Before evening they entered Rochefort. In the town and its environs were a regiment of naval artillery, fifteen hundred National Guards, and nearly three thousand gens d'armes, all of them well disposed toward the Emperor. They protested their devotion to him. They begged to follow him. He stayed at the Maritime Prefecture, and the people gave him just such a welcome as he had received at Niort. There was not a soldier within ten leagues who was not anxious to see him. "The people," says the Duke of Rovigo, an eyewitness, "never went from under the Emperor's windows; he was obliged to show himself at times to satisfy their impatience. Every time he did so he was received with the same respect as if he had triumphed over all his enemies. Rochefort is one of the towns on whose sanitation Napoleon had expended most money. For many years he had continued the works for drying up the marshes that surround it, and had also done much toward embellishing the town itself. All these undertakings had been crowned with success; the inhabitants of Rochefort were grateful on that account, and not afraid to show it."

Tuesday, July 4. Napoleon was soon to be forced to a decision. Up to June 29 there had been few English cruisers in sight, and those far away. But since that day they were approaching the two channels, the Brittany channel and that of Antioche, by which Rochefort communicates with the sea. In the roadstead lay two French men-of-war, the *Saale* and the *Méduse,* which the Provisional Government had put at the disposal of the Emperor to land him wherever he chose except on any part of the French coast, but they were now blockaded by English cruisers.

The situation constantly becoming more critical, Napoleon called a naval council in the morning of July 4, to consider it on all sides. Admiral Martin and Baron Bonnefoux, the maritime prefect, were present.

It was said at this council that, notwithstanding the approach of the English vessels, the two French frigates had the reputation of being such good sailers that, once outside the channels, they could elude all pursuit. Still, favorable winds would be required, and at present, unfortunately, they were contrary. Napoleon, who greatly dreaded leaving France, did not complain much at this delay. More occupied, probably, with what was passing at Paris than with events at Rochefort, he followed the confused accounts in the journals, in the hope of drawing from them some conclusion favorable to himself, or, at least, favorable to his son.

The maritime prefect wrote the following letter on July 4, to the Minister of the Navy: " Monseigneur, I have the honor to inform Your Excellency that Napoleon arrived at Rochefort yesterday, at nine in the morning, with his suite. The frigates were ready, but the English fleet stationed here, consisting of two ships, two frigates, two corvettes, and a small vessel, blockade the port, and every kind of transport from the Gironde to La Rochelle, so completely that there is neither hope of getting past them unperceived nor of forcing a way between them. The august personage whom the French nation has taken under its protection has made all his arrangements for departure. The intentions of the commission and the orders of Your Excellency will be executed in every point which concerns me. His Majesty is and will be treated with attention and respect due to his situation and to the crown which he has worn."

On the same day, the carriages which had left Malmaison when the Emperor did, and which carried Madame Bertrand, M. and Madame de Montholon, M. de Las Cases, and their children, as well as several orderly officers, arrived at Rochefort. In the evening King Joseph made his appearance.

Wednesday, July 5, to Friday, July 7. Listen to Count de Las Cases, an eyewitness: "At Rochefort the Emperor no longer wore a uniform. He lodged at the prefecture, and a great many people were constantly grouped about the house. From time to time cheers broke out; twice or thrice the Emperor made his appearance in the balcony. Many propositions were made to him by generals who came in person or sent special emissaries. For the rest, during his entire stay at Rochefort, the Emperor was precisely as he had been in the Tuileries; we did not approach him more freely; he received hardly any one except Bertrand and Savary, and we were reduced to rumors and conjectures concerning him. Always, it seems as if the Emperor, in the midst of whatever agitation of men and things, remains calm and impassible, shows himself very indifferent, and, above all, very little harassed."

In reality, Napoleon did not wish to depart until he knew the result of the political crisis which, at Paris, was reaching its height. He had still a lingering hope, so long as the army clung to the tricolor and Louis XVIII. had not re-entered the Tuileries. The Provisional Government and the two Chambers were in their agony. On July 3, a capitulation had been signed, in virtue of which the French army evacuated Paris, and retired across the Loire. The soldiers had in vain broken their weapons and exclaimed against this treason. On July 5, the enemy entered the capital as if it were a conquered city.

King Joseph, on his way to Rochefort, had seen the French columns marching towards the Loire. He had heard generals, officers, and soldiers ardently longing for the presence of the Emperor. This news agitated Napoleon greatly. On learning that the Army of the Loire would be raised to eighty thousand men, he recalled the miracles he had so often wrought with many less, both in the first Italian campaign and in that of 1814. Saying to himself that his abdication might be considered null, since no account had been made of his son's rights, he experienced a violent temptation to place himself once more at the head of the troops. But reflection showed him that France was weary of fighting; that all Europe would rise in arms against him, if he attempted to reappear upon the scene, and that he, the great Emperor, could not without loss descend to the part of a mere party chief. But what was he to do ? Where would he find a refuge ? How should he escape the English cruisers? How reach the United States?

Propositions, each more dangerous than the others, were constantly being made to the unfortunate Emperor. A French seaman, M. Besson, commanding a Danish merchant vessel, guaranteed to conceal him perfectly, and offered to start at once for the United States. He demanded nothing but a small sum, sufficient to idemnify the owners. A contract was signed, but Napoleon refused to hide himself in the hold of a neutral vessel. Such a lurking-place seemed to him unworthy of his glory.

Another proposition, suggested by Admiral Martin, was for him to go up the Seudre in a small boat, cross on horseback the tongue of land separating the Charente from the Gironde, and embark at Royan on a French corvette, commanded by Captain Baudin, a daring and distinguished seaman, who died an admiral of France. But it was feared that the corvette could not escape the British fleet.

Finally a small coasting-vessel was suggested. It was all ready to sail, and was to be manned by midshipmen who hoped to outwit the vigilance of the cruisers. But once at sea, this coaster would be suspected, and it was more than doubtful whether it was substantial enough to make a voyage like that from Rochefort to the United States.

Moreover, time was pressing. Louis XVIII. was about to reascend the throne, and his instructions against Napoleon would certainly be more rigorous than those of the Provisional Government. It was plain that Napoleon would not be permitted to profit by the French frigates, and would be in danger of becoming the King's prisoner.

Saturday, July 8. In the morning, General Beker observed respectfully to the Emperor that the time for delay was over. Napoleon decided, therefore, to leave Rochefort for the roadstead of the Island of Aix, where he could go on board the *Saale*, one of the two French frigates, and there await a favorable wind. That evening he started in a carriage for Fouras, which is at the mouth of the Charente, in the roadstead of Aix. The people, hearing of his departure, hastened to attend him on his journey. There was a considerable crowd when he alighted from the carriage at Fouras. All wore sad faces, and the whisper went round, "Is it possible that such a great man should be abandoned like this?"

The Emperor bade adieu to each one of the detachment of cavalry who had accompanied him, and got into the *Saale's* yawl, which had been waiting for him before the chateau of Fouras. The officers of his suite followed in the boats of the *Méduse*. It was late when he went aboard the *Saale*, the wind being contrary and very strong. He spent the night of July 8–9 on the ship.

Sunday, July 9. In the morning, as the winds

still remained contrary, the Emperor and his suite went to the Island of Aix. He visited the fortifications and reviewed the regiment of marines, who shouted, " Long live the Emperor! To the Army of Loire !" He went back to the *Saale* for breakfast. During the day the winds became more favorable, but the English fleet seemed to be watching the French frigates. In the evening Napoleon, feeling inclined to return to Rochefort, embarked in a small boat, so as to be less noticed; but as the shore seemed guarded, he went back to the Island of Aix. He was blockaded on this island, without means of egress either toward the continent or the sea. Proposals for a clandestine flight were again renewed; but he continued to reject the idea of embarking on a coasting-vessel. Among other reasons he assigned that of the necessity of revictualling on the coast of Spain or Portugal, which would expose him to fall into the hands of a powerful enemy. The Danish corvette was also suggested. As it was certain that she would be searched by the English as soon as she quitted the port, the Emperor was assured that a hiding-place could be contrived for him. It was a cask to be stowed among the ballast, and provided with tubes for introducing air. But the extreme rigor with which the search would doubtless be made, and the corpulence of Napoleon, which would not permit of his remaining any length of time closely confined in such an uncomfortable position, caused this expedient to be rejected: besides, the Emperor refused it as undignified.

The danger continued to increase. The white flag
was about to be raised at Rochefort. Already the
commandant of the place had caused Napoleon to be
notified, as respectfully as possible, that he must
think seriously of departing. The Provisional Government was no longer in existence. The hall of
the Chamber of Deputies had been closed by the
Prussians. On July 8, Louis XVIII., escorted by
the Marshal Dukes of Tarento, Ragusa, Feltre, Reg-
gio, and Belluno, had triumphantly re-entered the
Tuileries. Napoleon could foresee that he would
not be protected by the batteries of the Island of Aix
much longer. He could no longer expect any consideration on the part of France. And then it was
that the idea came to him of confiding himself to the
generosity of England.

Monday, July 10. In the night of July 9–10, Napoleon sent the Duke of Rovigo and Count de Las
Cases to the commander of the English fleet, Captain
Maitland, who was on board the man-of-war *Beller-*
ophon. The two messengers of the Emperor left
the *Saale* in a small schooner, availing themselves
of the outgoing tide, which carried them beyond
Point Chassiron, at the extremity of the Island of
Oleron, where the English vessel was cruising about
in company with the corvette *Myrmidon.*

The two envoys went on board the *Bellerophon*
about eight in the morning. M. de Las Cases apprised Captain Maitland of some news of which he
was still in ignorance, namely: that in consequence

of the events which had followed the battle of Waterloo, the Emperor had abdicated and come to Rochefort with the intention of sailing for America; that the Provisional Government had demanded passports for him from Wellington, who had referred the request to London; and that it was thought they might have been forwarded to the English fleet, stationed near Rochefort. Captain Maitland replied that he had received nothing. M. de Las Cases returned that the Emperor, having completely terminated his political career, desired to go away peaceably; and that if he was anxious for passports, it was because he desired to prevent an engagement between the two French frigates and such Britannic vessels as they might meet.

" I was entirely ignorant of the details you have given me," replied Captain Maitland. " I had heard of nothing but the victory at Waterloo. Consequently, I cannot answer the request which is the subject of your message. But if you will wait a few moments, I shall probably know more about it, for I see a corvette trying to come up to us. She signals that she comes from England and has letters for me. I shall handle the vessel so as to make her approach easier, and meantime we will go to breakfast." The corvette was the *Falmouth*, which did, in fact, come from England, and had passed through the Bay of Quiberon, whence it brought despatches from Admiral Hotham.

Savary and Las Cases were eating breakfast with

Captain Maitland when the captain of the *Falmouth* reached the *Bellerophon*. After learning the contents of Admiral Hotham's despatches, Maitland said: " There is not a word concerning what you have just told me; I know, even, that when the *Falmouth* sailed they knew nothing about it in England."

The conversation was very courteous on both sides. Captain Maitland spoke French well. He was an honorable seaman, and a man of good breeding, who seemed to respect Napoleon's misfortunes.

He ended by saying to his two interlocutors: " I should like to be able to satisfy you, but you see I cannot. I am going to notify my Admiral, who is in the Bay of Quiberon, of your coming on board. At the same time I will send him the letter you brought me from General Bertrand, and let you know his answer as soon as I receive it."

Las Cases replied: " The Emperor does not want to steal away clandestinely. Personally, he has no motive for doing so, as the application we have just made on his behalf sufficiently proves. But if, before your response arrives, the wind should become favorable, and, desiring to profit by it, he goes out on the French frigates, what will you do? What will you do if, instead of the French frigates, he goes in a French merchant vessel? In fine, if instead of doing either, he should sail in a neutral vessel, an American ship for instance, what will you do?"

Captain Maitland responded: " If the Emperor

goes on the French frigates, I will attack them and take them if I can: in that case the Emperor will be a prisoner. If he goes in a French merchant vessel, as we are at war, I will take the vessel, and again the Emperor will be a prisoner. If he goes in a neutral vessel, and I search it, I could not take it on me to let him pass. I should hold on to him and refer the matter to my Admiral, who would decide it."

These responses once made, the conversation between Napoleon's two envoys and the English sailor went on with great politeness. "The Emperor," said the latter, "did rightly in asking for passports, in order to escape the disagreeable encounters which would be constantly renewed at sea; but I do not believe our government would let him go to America." "Where do they propose that he should go, then?" asked Savary. "I cannot guess," replied Maitland; "but I am almost certain of what I just told you. What repugnance would he have against coming to England? All difficulties could be obviated in that way."

To the objections made by the two envoys in view of the English climate and the national ill-will toward Napoleon, Captain Maitland replied nearly in these terms: "It is a mistake to think the English climate is bad and damp. There are counties where it is as mild as that of France; Kent, for instance. As to the charms of social life, they are incomparably superior in England to anything the Emperor could find in America. And as to the ill-feeling which he might fear, to come to England would be the very way to extinguish it. Living in the midst of the nation and under the protection of the laws, he would be defended from everybody and would render the efforts of his enemies powerless. Even if the Ministry wished to annoy him, which I do not believe, they could not, because our government is not arbitrary; it is subjected to the laws. I am persuaded that the government would take the proper measures to assure the Emperor's tranquillity and that of the place where he should reside; such, for example, as were taken with regard to his brother Lucien. But I cannot conceive it possible that it could go beyond that; for, as I have told you, the Ministers would have no right, and the nation would not allow it."

Las Cases replied: "I am not empowered to treat that question with you. But I shall remember all you have said, and will report it to the Emperor. In case he should adopt the idea of going to England, — and I will do all in my power to persuade him, — may he count on being taken on board your vessel with all those who accompany him, this supposition debarring him from taking passage on the French frigates?"

Captain Maitland answered: "I will ask instructions from my Admiral. But if, before they reach me, the Emperor comes and asks a passage on board my ship, I will receive him. Moreover, I am going into the roadstead of the Basques, where I shall be nearer you, and where you can communicate with me whenever you please."

Las Cases and Savary, satisfied with Captain Maitland's courteous treatment, but not building many hopes on British generosity, took their leave, and, going on board the schooner which brought them, returned to the Emperor. He had remained on board the *Saale* in the roadstead of the Island of Aix. He meditated all the evening on the report they brought him.

Tuesday, July 11. In the night of July 10–11, Napoleon ordered Savary to go and tell Captain Philibert, commander of the *Saale,* to sail at once. The latter replied that he had secret orders; he was forbidden to accomplish his mission, "if the frigates ran into any danger." "So then," exclaimed Savary, "all this was a mere deception; the only aim of the Provisional Government was to place the Emperor under the necessity of delivering himself to the enemy!" "I do not know," replied Captain Philibert, "but I have orders not to sail." Savary, in consternation, brought this answer to Napoleon. "My presentiments warned me of it," said the Emperor, sadly, "and yet I was unwilling to believe it."

Then Captain Ponée, who commanded the other French frigate, the *Méduse,* made a heroic proposition. He offered to weigh anchor at sunset, when there was usually a favorable breeze, and attack the *Bellerophon,* remaining attached to her side, until, even at the sacrifice of the *Méduse,* he should have made it impossible for her to move. Meantime, the *Saale,* with the Emperor on board, could gain the open sea. Napoleon, profoundly moved by such devotion, declined this offer, which the dispositions of Captain Philibert made impracticable in any case. He had no longer anything to hope for from the two French frigates, the *Méduse* and the *Saale*.

Wednesday, July 12. Napoleon received a visit from his brother Joseph, and letters announcing the events at Paris. There was more to be feared from the victorious emigrés than from the English themselves. Departure had become indispensable. Of all solutions, that of falling alive into the hands of the Royalists would be the worst. They would not pardon the Emperor the fright they had experienced during the Hundred Days. The moment that he could hope nothing farther from the two French frigates, Napoleon left the *Saale*, and had himself put ashore on the Island of Aix, where a regiment of naval infantry were constantly in garrison. He was received there with enthusiasm. Still, it was necessary to decide on something. To go up the Seudre in a boat, and cross the tongue of land separating the Charente from the Gironde on horseback, in order to embark on an American vessel at the mouth of the latter stream, was no longer practicable ; for, since the last news from Paris, the white flag was floating everywhere, and the Royalist population would prevent his embarkation. Besides, the winds were still unfavorable.

Thursday, July 13. Despairing of his cause, Napoleon, who at bottom had no confidence in British generosity, was tempted to accept the offer of two coasting-vessels. The intrepid midshipmen said to him: " Sire, we are resolute men ; confide yourself to us. By oars or by sail we will take the boats beyond the channels; after that we will trust ourselves to the winds. They may bring us into the way of some merchant vessel which we will seize, and which we will oblige to transport Your Majesty to the United States. Under cover of the night, and with our oars, we can slip out unperceived." Napoleon was going to allow himself to be persuaded. In the evening of July 13, the two coasters were brought to the anchorage of Aix. Already several of the Emperor's attendants had entered it, when suddenly those who were about to start, and still more those who were to be left behind, broke into an indescribable explosion of grief. The women sobbed. Napoleon could not endure this spectacle. " Well ! " he cried, " let us be done with it and give ourselves up to the English, since after all we cannot in any way escape them." And he thanked the brave young men, whose devotion and enthusiasm had profoundly touched him.

Friday, July 14. So this man, of whom one could have said that the whole world was not enough for him (*Æstuat infelix angusto in carcere mundi*), this conqueror who had not treated with Europe to preserve the Hanseatic Towns, the modern Cæsar, the new Charlemagne, the Emperor of the French, the King of Italy, the mediator of the Swiss Confedera tion, the protector of the Confederation of the Rhine, now banned, proscribed, tracked like a wild beast, chased from the earth and from the sea, had no longer a stone on which to lay his head!

In the morning of July 14, the Emperor once more sent Count de Las Cases on board the *Bellerophon*, accompanied this time by General Lallemand. The two envoys asked Captain Maitland if he had received yet any response from his superior, Admiral Hotham, chief of the naval station. He replied in the negative, but declared that he was, nevertheless, ready to receive the Emperor on the *Bellerophon*, and take him to England. " It is my private opinion," added he, " that Napoleon will find there all the respect and good treatment which he can desire. It is a country where the Prince and the Ministers do not exercise arbitrary authority. The English people have a generosity of sentiment and a liberality of opinion which are superior to sovereignty itself." Captain Maitland, however, spoke for himself only, and made no engagement on behalf of the British government, whose official intentions he did not know. At this time the *Bellerophon* was rejoined by the English corvette, the *Slany*, commanded by Captain Sertorius.

Las Cases and General Lallemand returned the same day to the Island of Aix, and repeated to the Emperor what Captain Maitland had said. Evidently there was only one of two things for him to do : to deliver himself up to the English, or to attempt to rejoin the Army of the Loire in order to begin a civil war, without the least chance of success. Napoleon caused all those who had accompanied him to be summoned, and asked their opinion. They were almost unanimous in saying that he ought to confide himself to England. Then the Emperor said : " If it were a question of marching to the conquest of an empire, or of saving one, I might attempt a return to the Island of Elba ; but I desire nothing but repose. And if I were again the cause of even a single discharge of cannon, spite would profit by the circumstance to destroy me. I am offered repose in England. I do not know the Prince Regent, but from what I have been told, I cannot distrust the loyalty of his character. My decision is made. I am going to write to him ; and to-morrow, at daybreak, we will go on board the English vessel."

All retired to make their preparations for departure. It was then Napoleon wrote to the Prince Regent of England the letter which will be famous for all time : —

" ROYAL HIGHNESS : Exposed to the factions which divide my country, and to the enmity of the greatest European Powers, I have ended my political career, and am going, like Themistocles, to sit down beside the hearths of the British people. I place myself under the protection of their laws, which I claim from Your Royal Highness, as the most powerful, the most constant, and the most generous of my enemies."

General Gourgaud was charged with carrying the memorable letter to the Prince Regent, and received the following instructions: —

" My aide-de-camp Gourgaud will present himself on board the English squadron with Count de Las Cases. According to the instructions he receives from the commander of this squadron, he will go either to the admiral or to London. He will try to obtain an audience of the Prince Regent, and deliver my letter to him. If there is no inconvenience in giving me passports to the United States of America, that is what I desire; but I do not want them to go to any colony. If America is impossible, I prefer England to any other country. I will assume the title of Colonel Muiron or Duroc. If I am to go to England, I would like to live in a country house, ten or twelve leagues from London, where I am anxious to arrive in the strictest possible disguise. The house should be large enough to accommodate all my servants. I am desirous to avoid London, and in this the government would doubtless agree with me. If the Ministry desire to place a commissary near me, Gourgaud will take care that this shall carry with it no appearance of captivity, and that he shall be a man whose rank and character cannot possibly give occasion for evil thoughts. If Gourgaud is to go to the admiral, it would be better for the captain to keep him on board until he can be sent in a corvette, so as to be sure to reach London before us.

" NAPOLEON.

" Island of Aix, July 14, 1815."

Las Cases, accompanied by General Gourgaud, started about four o'clock in the afternoon for the *Bellerophon*. His mission was to announce that the Emperor would come on board the next morning, and to give Captain Maitland a copy of Napoleon's letter to the Prince Regent. This letter, worthy of one of Plutarch's heroes, was greatly admired by the English seaman, who allowed two other captains to take copies of it, under the seal of privacy until it should be made public. He despatched General Gourgaud at once to London on the corvette *Slany*. But hardly had this vessel started, when Maitland, his face and voice greatly altered, exclaimed : " Count de Las Cases, I have been tricked. When I am treating with you, when I am depriving myself of a corvette, I am told that Napoleon has just escaped. That will put me in a frightful predicament with my government."

Las Cases gave a start. What would he not have given that the news were true ! But it was not. " At what hour is it pretended that the Emperor got off ? " he asked Captain Maitland. " At noon." " Reassure yourself ; I left the Emperor at the Island of Aix this afternoon, at four o'clock." " You positively declare that to me ? " " I give you my word."

Turning to some officers near by, Captain Maitland said to them in English: " The news must be false. Count de Las Cases is too calm. He looks too honest, and besides, he has just given me his word of honor."

Nothing further was said except in relation to the next day. " Would you like me to send my boats for the Emperor ? " asked Maitland. " No," returned Las Cases. " The separation is already too painful to the French seamen. We must leave them the satisfaction of guarding the Emperor up to the last minute."

Saturday, July 15. In the morning, Napoleon was beginning to dress when General Beker hurried in to announce that an emissary had just arrived at Rochefort commissioned to arrest him. There was not a single minute to lose. At daybreak, Napoleon, at last making up his mind to go, went down to the shore, and after receiving the sad farewells of a pitying throng, embarked with his companions in the vessels which took them to the brig *Epervier*, whence they were to go on board the *Bellerophon*.

Before entering the *Epervier* the Emperor bade adieu to General Beker, for whom he had only words of praise, and who wept. "General," said he, "I thank you for your noble and delicate conduct. Why did I know you so late? You ought never to have left my person. Be happy, and transmit to France the expression of my good wishes." The General begged to be allowed to go with him as far as the *Bellerophon*. "No," replied the Emperor. "I do not know what the English have in store for me; but if they betray my confidence, it will be said that you delivered me to my enemies."

Profiting by the low tide to get out of the roadstead of Aix and into that of the Basques, where the

Bellerophon lay at anchor, Napoleon reached the ship with difficulty, because the weather was too calm. Captain Maitland, full of impatience, was sweeping the horizon with his glass to see whether the illustrious captive was approaching. He sent a yawl to meet him, and the Emperor got into it from the brig *Epervier.* From that moment he ceased to be a free man; he became the prisoner of his most implacable enemies. On board the *Epervier* there was a prolonged groaning, broken by cries of "Long live the Emperor!" All the sailors wept, and kept their eyes fixed on the great man who was boarding the *Bellerophon.*

XIV.

THE BELLEROPHON.

WHEN the Emperor came aboard the *Bellero-phon*, Las Cases, who was at the ladder, presented Captain Maitland. Napoleon, raising his hat, said in a firm voice, "I come on board your ship to put myself under the protection of the laws of England." Captain Maitland, after having introduced his officers, conducted the Emperor to his cabin, of which he put him in possession. The Emperor was accompanied by Generals Bertrand, Savary, Lallemand, and Montholon, Count de Las Cases and his son, and the Countesses Bertrand and Montholon. The first of these ladies had three children with her; the second had one. To these must be added nine officers of inferior rank and thirty-nine domestics. The principal personages were received on the *Bellerophon*, the others on the corvette *Myrmidon*, commanded by Captain Gambier.

Toward three in the afternoon the *Superb*, a seventy-four-gun ship, commanded by Admiral Hotham, entered the anchorage. It had come from the roadstead of Quiberon into that of the Basques.

The Admiral visited the Emperor on board the *Bellerophon*, and begged that he would honor him by breakfasting on the *Superb* the following day with all his suite. Napoleon accepted.

Sunday, July 16, 1815. Let us leave the account to Las Cases: " As he started, in the morning, to go on board Admiral Hotham's ship, the Emperor stopped short on the bridge of the *Bellerophon* before the soldiers drawn up in his honor. He made them go through their drill several times, and as their manner of charging bayonets was not precisely like that of the French, he went quickly into the midst of the soldiers, pushing aside their bayonets with his two hands, and seized a musket from one in the rear rank, with which he performed the evolution himself in our fashion. A sudden change of expression appeared on the faces of the soldiers, the officers, and all the spectators : it expressed their astonishment at seeing the Emperor place himself thus in the midst of English bayonets, some of which touched his breast. This circumstance made a vivid impression." Napoleon drilling English soldiers on board the *Bellerophon* — would not that be a good subject for a military picture?

Afterwards, the Emperor went on board the *Superb*. The ship was in full dress. The bridge was covered with a richly decorated tent canopied with the English standard. Ordinary labors on the vessel were intermitted. A fine band was playing on the poop. The sailors in uniform were on the yards. Admiral

Hotham presented each of his officers by name to the Emperor. This ceremony over, he showed him the batteries and then offered him an extremely well-served breakfast. Afterwards he proposed to him to remain on the *Superb*, which was larger and more commodious than the *Bellerophon*. Napoleon refused this offer out of good feeling, not wishing to pain Captain Maitland, whose kindness he appreciated: he returned the same day to the *Bellerophon*.

Monday, July 17. The *Bellerophon* and the corvette *Myrmidon* weighed anchor and made sail for England. The winds were poor, and they did not lose sight of land.

Tuesday, July 18, *to Saturday, July* 22. The voyage was slow. It was with difficulty that they got into the English Channel in going up the French coast. Napoleon appeared gentle and affable. His calmness and the equability of his temper gained the approbation of everybody. He used to stay on deck for the greater part of the day, conversing at length with Captain Maitland, seizing occasions to say agreeable things, and talking of the English navy, whose skill he admired, and the English army, whose rare steadfastness he praised. He spoke also, and with great affection, of his wife and son, complaining of his separation from them; he showed their portraits to Captain Maitland, with tears in his eyes. His health was good, but he was subject to drowsiness. Captain, officers, and crew had all speedily adopted toward him the same manners that were observed by his suite; the same deference, the same language, the same respect. The Captain always addressed him as Sire or Majesty. Whenever he came on the bridge, every one removed his hat. No one was admitted to his table except at his invitation.

Sunday, July 23. Toward four in the morning they sighted Ushant, which had been passed during the night. More than once the Emperor glanced sadly toward the coast of France, but he did not say a word. As they approached the Channel, English vessels were seen coming and going in all directions. By night England was in sight.

Monday, July 24. Toward eight in the morning they weighed anchor in the roadstead of Torbay. Alas! it was not thus that, in the time when he camped at Boulogne, Napoleon had hoped to descend on the English coast! From the poop of the *Bellerophon* he looked at the shore and the anchorage of the vessel. On entering the roadstead, which is very picturesque, "This reminds me," said he, "of Porto-Ferrajo and the Island of Elba." Very soon afterwards, General Gourgaud presented himself. He had left Aix on the corvette *Slany*, to carry a letter to the Prince Regent, but had not been able to discharge the commission: he had been obliged to give up the letter, and was not even permitted to land. This was a bad omen.

Napoleon did not go ashore. He remained on board the *Bellerophon* in the road of Torbay. The ship had scarcely cast anchor when Captain Maitland received despatches from Lord Keith, Admiral of the Channel fleet, and shortly after from the Board of Admiralty, which enjoined him not to permit any one, no matter of what rank or station, to be on board the *Bellerophon*, excepting the officers and sailors composing its crew. As soon as the Emperor's presence in the bay was made known, a crowd of small boats filled with curious people began to make their appearance.

Tuesday, July 25. Napoleon was struck with the multitude of persons in boats crowding about the ship in the hope of getting sight of him. He looked at them from his cabin, and sometimes went out on the bridge. No one suspected, as yet, the sorrowful fate which awaited the great man. Captain Maitland received a letter from Lord Keith, in which the following passage occurs: "Say to the Emperor that I should be glad if he would let me know what would be agreeable to him; I would willingly attend to it. Thank him on my behalf for the generous attentions he himself gave to my nephew, who was taken to him a prisoner after being wounded at Waterloo."

Wednesday, July 26. During the night of July 25–26, the *Bellerophon* received orders to leave Torbay for Plymouth. Having weighed anchor very early, they arrived in the roadstead of that city at about four in the afternoon. Sinister presentiments began to circulate. Armed boats surrounded the ship, which was not visited by Admiral Keith, although he was in the bay. At the moment when two English frigates cast anchor, one on either side of the *Bellerophon*, some one said in a whisper to Las Cases: " You see these frigates? In the night they will carry off the Emperor and you, and sail for Saint Helena."

Listen to this faithful courtier of misfortune: " No, never," he exclaims, " can I render the effect of these terrible words! A cold sweat broke out on my body; it was an unexpected sentence of death. Pitiless executioners had seized me for the torture; I was to be torn violently from all that attached me to life; sadly I extended my arms to all I held dear; it was in vain; perish I must. This thought and an unruly crowd of others raised a veritable tempest in me: it was the laceration of a soul seeking to free itself from its terrestrial alloy! It whitened my hair. . . . Happily the crisis was brief, and my soul came out victorious, — so entirely victorious that, from that moment, I felt myself superior to all that men could do. I felt that thereafter I could defy injustice, ill-treatment, torture. I swore, above all, that no one should ever hear from me either complaints or petitions. But let not those among us, to whom I must have seemed tranquil in these fatal circumstances, accuse me of a want of feeling! Their agony was prolonged and in detail; mine came all at once."

As usual, the Emperor made his appearance on the bridge. His face betrayed neither emotion nor uneasiness.

Thursday, July 27. Again we leave the word to Las Cases: "It would be difficult to describe," he says, "our anxieties and torments: the greater number of us seemed hardly to be living; the least circumstance from land, the most commonplace opinion of any one on board, the least authentic article, supplied us with subjects for the gravest arguments and caused continual oscillations between hope and fear. We sought to get favorable versions and deceitful anticipations from any one whatever, so little do the expansion and mobility of our national character incline us to that stoical resignation and impassible concentration which flow only from settled ideas and positive doctrine imbibed in childhood.

"The public journals, the ministerial ones especially, were let loose against us; it was the halloo of the ministers preparing for the blow they meant to strike. It would not be easy to get an idea of the horrors, the lies, the imprecations, which piled up against us; and it is well known that such things make an impression on the multitude, no matter how well disposed they may be. Hence the manners of those around us began to stiffen, their politeness seemed embarrassed, and their faces dubious."

The Emperor maintained an imperturbable tranquillity. His presence in the Bay of Plymouth produced a prodigious effect. He was going to excite throughout all England a sentiment of curiosity which amounted to frenzy. People came in crowds, as if on a pilgrimage, in the hope of seeing for an instant the features of the legendary man. There were not horses enough on the road between London and Plymouth, so great was the throng of travellers who wanted to be able to say one day to their children: " I have seen Napoleon!"

Friday, July 28. As he beheld the innumerable boats which pressed around the *Bellerophon*, the Emperor, in the very midst of his misfortunes, had an intuition of his future glory. He perceived that his adversity, like his former power, would assume epic proportions, and that all poets would celebrate him.

Listen to a Frenchman, Count de Las Cases, and to an Englishman, Walter Scott, who both describe this eager thronging of the English people about the glorious captive.

" It was known," says Las Cases, " that the Emperor always came out on the bridge toward five o'clock. Some time beforehand the boats began to close in beside each other. There were thousands of them, and so close together that not a glimpse could be caught of the sea; one might rather have believed that this crowd of spectators had assembled in some public square. On the appearance of the Emperor, the noises, the movements, the gestures, of so many people presented a singular spectacle. At the same time it was easy to see that there was nothing hostile in all this; if curiosity had brought them, interest would accompany them home. One could even see that this sentiment visibly increased. At first they were content to look; afterwards they saluted; some kept their hats off; and sometimes they cheered. Even our emblems began to make their appearance: women and young men would arrive adorned with carnations."

. And now hear Walter Scott: "That popular curiosity, bordering on fury, which prevails in all free states, but which seems carried to the greatest excess by the English nation, caused the sea around the *Bellerophon* to be covered with such a multitude of barks that in spite of the peremptory orders of the Admiralty and the efforts of the coast-guard vessels, it was almost impossible to keep them at the prescribed distance from the vessel, which was a cable's length. The persons on these boats ran the risk of sinking and of being killed (at least they might fear it, for several shots were fired to intimidate them): they exposed themselves, in a word, to all the dangers of a naval combat, rather than lose the opportunity of seeing the Emperor, of whom they had so often heard. When he appeared, he was received with acclamations, to which he responded by salutes; but he could not avoid displaying his surprise at the excess of a curiosity which he had never seen manifest itself with so much vivacity."

Saturday, July 29. The crowd of curious spectators was even greater than on the previous day. Thousands of small crafts surrounded the *Bellerophon* and passed hours in the roadstead, running against each other and exposed to grave dangers.

Sunday, July 30. One of the under-secretaries of

State, Sir Henry Bunbury, arrived from London. He brought the definite resolutions of the English government.

Monday, July 31. Lord Keith and Sir Henry Bunbury came on board the *Bellerophon*, and, in the name of the English Ministry, acquainted Napoleon with the following communication : —

" As it may be agreeable to General Buonaparte to learn, without further delay, the intentions of the British Government in his case, Your Lordship will communicate the subjoined information to him : It would be little in conformity with our duties towards our country and the Allied Powers, for us to leave General Buonaparte the means or the opportunity to trouble again the peace of Europe. This is why it becomes absolutely necessary that he should be restrained in his personal liberty, so far as this first and important object may require. The Island of Saint Helena has been selected for his future residence. Its climate is healthy, and its situation will permit of his being treated with more indulgence than could be shown elsewhere, in view of the indispensable precaution which would be necessary to secure his person. General Buonaparte is permitted to choose among those who accompanied him to England, with the exception of Generals Savary and Lallemand, three officers who, together with his surgeon, will be permitted to accompany him to Saint Helena, and cannot leave the island without the sanction of the British Government. Rear-Admiral Sir

George Cockburn, who is named commander-in-chief of the Cape of Good Hope and the adjacent seas, will conduct General Buonaparte and his suite to Saint Helena, and will receive detailed instructions concerning the execution of the service. Sir George Cockburn will probably be ready to start in a few days; for this reason it is desirable that General Buonaparte should, without delay, make choice of the persons who are to accompany him."

This painful document was read aloud in French by Sir Henry Bunbury. Napoleon listened to it without any sign of emotion or impatience. When it was ended, he was asked, like a condemned man to whom his sentence has just been read, whether he had any observations to make. Then he began to speak quietly, declaring, with great coolness, that he protested solemnly against the orders just read; that the English Ministry had no right to dispose in this way of his person; that he appealed to the nation and the laws, and asked to what tribunal he should carry this appeal. "I came," said he, "to confide myself voluntarily to the hospitality of your nation. I am not a prisoner of war; and even if I were, I should have a right to be treated according to the law of nations. I came as a passenger on one of your vessels, after preliminary negotiations with its commander. If he had told me I would be made a prisoner, I should not have come. I asked him if he would receive me on board and carry me to England. He answered yes, having received, or pretending to have received, precise orders from his government. Was it then a trap you were laying for me? I went aboard an English vessel as I would have entered an English town: a vessel, a village, it is all the same thing. As to Saint Helena, it would be my death sentence. . . . I could not live there three months. I am accustomed to walk twenty miles a day. What would become of me on that little rock at the end of the world? No; Botany Bay is preferable to Saint Helena. And what good would my death do you? I am no longer a sovereign. What danger could arise from my living as a private person in the interior of England, subject to such restrictions as the government should deem suitable ? ''

Lord Keith and Sir Henry Bunbury made no remark, save to call the Emperor's attention to the fact that their mission was solely to communicate to him the document to which he had just listened.

Napoleon proceeded without interruption, insisting on his preference for England and his desire to intrust himself to it rather than to any other nation. "Otherwise," said he, "why should I not have gone to my father-in-law, or to the Emperor Alexander, who is my personal friend? We fell out because he wanted to annex Poland, and my popularity with the Poles embarrassed him. But in other respects he was my friend, and he would not have treated me in this fashion. If your government acts in this way, it will disgrace you in the eyes of Europe. Your people themselves will blame it. You do not know, moreover, what a sensation my death would cause, both in France and Italy. At present they have a high opinion of England in both those countries. If you kill me, that opinion will be destroyed, and many English lives will pay for mine. Who could have forced me to the step I took? The tricolor was still floating at Bordeaux, Nantes, and Rochefort. The army has not even yet made its submission. Very well; if I had preferred to remain in France, who could have prevented me from remaining concealed there for years in the midst of a people so attached to me?"

Then, recalling his glory and past splendors: "Remember," said he, "what I have been and what place I have taken among European sovereigns. This one solicited my protection; that one gave me his daughter; all sought for my friendship. I was recognized as Emperor by all the Powers of Europe, England excepted, and that recognized me as First Consul. Your government has no right to style me *General Buonaparte.* I am either Prince or Consul. I should be treated as such, and not otherwise. When I was at Elba, I was as much a sovereign in that island as Louis XVIII. was in France. We had our respective flags, our vessels, and our troops. Mine were less numerous, it is true. I had six hundred men, and he had two hundred thousand. Finally, I made war on him. I was defeated and dethroned. That affords no excuse for depriving me of my rank as a European sovereign."

Napoleon concluded by saying: "No! no! I will not go to Saint Helena. I am not a Hercules, but you will not take me there. I prefer death here, even. You found me free; send me back, replace me in the same condition, or let me go to America."

A legitimist historian, M. Alfred Nettement, thus appreciates Napoleon's remarks: "Several things are to be considered in these words of the Emperor. In the first place, the discernment, the calculation, with which he prepares the rôle he wishes to play in history. His letter, graven in marble by that character of antique grandeur which he knew how to give his style, is written for posterity, who will read it over the Regent's shoulder. In reality, the Emperor made use in an inevitable action (for he had been the prisoner of England from the time he went to the Island of Aix) of that supreme art which, in the days of his power, he knew how to impress on all he did; like the antique gladiator, he draped himself when falling. Nor is this all. At the moment when he loses his sword in his implacable duel with England, he recommences by speech that duel which he will continue with the pen on the rock of Saint Helena, in dedicating England to the execration of posterity. The anathema, to which he will add each day a malediction and an accusing groan, begins on the *Bellerophon*. But what is most instructive and finest in his words is that tardy appeal to law, to justice, and to equity, an appeal full of lessons in the mouth of the man of force and absolute power."

After his interview with Lord Keith and Sir Henry Bunbury, Napoleon showed himself as usual on the bridge. He was absolutely calm. But despair overcame his unfortunate companions. Generals Savary and Lallemand, excluded from the amnesty by the government of Louis XVIII., who reserved them for punishment like Ney and Labédoyère, interpreted in the most sinister way the refusal to allow them to accompany the Emperor to Saint Helena. They were persuaded that England would deliver them to the French Royalists, who would destroy them.

Tuesday, August 1. The crowd of boats which followed each other continually into the bay, and which never numbered less than a thousand at a time, were held with difficulty at the prescribed distance from the *Bellerophon*, by the vessels ordered to prevent them, by force if necessary, from coming nearer. This multitude alarmed the English naval authorities, especially since Napoleon had declared he would not go to Saint Helena: they were afraid he might try to escape. Two frigates were sent to watch and protect the *Bellerophon*. The sentinels were doubled and tripled by day and night.

The members of the Emperor's suite observed the same etiquette with him as in the Tuileries. Grand Marshal Bertrand and General Savary, Duke of Rovigo, alone saw him habitually. There were some who had hardly approached him since they left Paris, nor spoken to him more frequently than if he were still living in an imperial palace.

In the evening, M. de Las Cases was translating the English newspapers to Napoleon when General Bertrand's wife, without having been summoned, and without having herself announced, suddenly rushed into the Emperor's cabin. She was beside herself. "Sire," she cried, "do not go to Saint Helena. Do not take away my husband." Napoleon's calmness troubled her still more. She went out as precipitately as she had entered. A few moments later great cries were heard and a movement of the crew, who were running noisily toward the stern of the ship. Madame Bertrand had tried to throw herself overboard.

Wednesday, August 2. M. de Las Cases learned that Napoleon had chosen him as one of his companions to Saint Helena. The Duke of Rovigo repeated to him Napoleon's kindly words. Las Cases says: "Savary loved the Emperor sincerely; I knew his heart, his soul, his uprightness; he seemed to me capable of true friendship. We should, doubtless, have been intimately united. May he never understand the sentiments and the regrets he has bequeathed me."

Thursday, August 3. In the evening the Emperor caused Las Cases to be summoned. "What good could Saint Helena be?" said he. "Would it be possible to support life there? After all, is it certain that I shall go? Is a man dependent on other men when he chooses not to be so? . . . My dear fellow, sometimes I long to leave you, and it would not be difficult. All that would be necessary would be to get a little excited and I should soon escape. All would be over, and you could quietly rejoin your families."

Doubtless Napoleon forgot at this moment that order of the day of Floréal 22, Year X., in which he had said, apropos of the suicide of a soldier of the Consular Guard : —

" The First Consul decrees that it shall be put on the regulations of the Guard that a soldier ought to know how to subdue the suffering and the melancholy of the passions; and that there is as much true courage in enduring with constancy the pains of the soul as remaining steadfast on the ramparts of a fortress. To abandon one's self to chagrin without resistance, to kill one's self in order to get rid of it, is to quit the field of battle before having conquered."

Las Cases vigorously combated the idea of suicide which seemed to tempt the Emperor. He developed in eloquent language the noblest considerations. Poets and philosophers had declared that to see a man struggling with misfortune is a spectacle worthy of the gods. Reverses and steadfastness have alike their glory; a character so noble and grand as that of Napoleon could not lower itself to the level of the most vulgar souls; he who had governed with so much splendor, who had been admired by the world and controlled its destinies, must not end like a despairing gamester or a deceived lover. What would become in that case of those who believed and hoped in him? Was not the extreme longing dis-

played by such persons a sufficient motive for endur-
ance? Moreover, who could penetrate into the secrets
of time? Who would dare affirm anything about
the future?

Napoleon replied: "Some things you say are interesting. But what could we do at Saint Helena, that
desolate spot?" "Sire, we would live in the past;
there is enough in it to satisfy us. Do we not enjoy
the lines of Cæsar and Alexander? We shall have
something better still: you will re-peruse your career,
Sire." "Well, yes; you are right; we will write our
memoirs. Yes, we must get to work: work also is
the scythe of time. After all, we must fulfil our
destiny: that is my great doctrine." And regaining
from that moment an easy and even cheerful aspect,
the Emperor turned the conversation to matters
entirely unconnected with his existing situation.

Friday, August 4. In the night of August 3–4,
the captain of the *Bellerophon* received orders to sail
early the next morning. They got under way and
sailed eastward up the Channel. The *Bellerophon*
was too old a ship for such a voyage as that to
Saint Helena, and besides she lacked the necessary
stores. They were to rejoin another vessel.

During the day the Emperor wrote the following
protest: "I solemnly protest here, before Heaven and
men, against the violation of my most sacred rights
and the use of force in disposing of my person.
I came freely on board the *Bellerophon;* I am not
the prisoner, but the guest, of England. I came at

the instigation of the captain, who said he had orders
to receive me on board and take me to England if
that were agreeable to me. I presented myself in
good faith. Seated on the deck of the *Bellerophon*,
I was at the fireside of the British people. If, in
giving the captain of the *Bellerophon* orders to receive
me and my suite, the government intended to lay an
ambush for me, it has forfeited its honor and tar-
nished its flag. This act once consummated, it will
be in vain for the English to boast hereafter of
their loyalty, their laws, and their liberty. British
faith will have perished in the hospitality of the
Bellerophon. I appeal from it to history; she will
say that an enemy who had fought the English
people for twenty years went of his own accord,
when in misfortune, to seek asylum under the protection of their laws. What more striking proof
could he have given of his esteem and confidence?
But how did the English respond to such magnanimity? They pretended to extend a hospitable hand
to this enemy; and when he had taken it in good
faith, they immolated him.   NAPOLEON.

"On board the *Bellerophon.* At sea."

What struck Chateaubriand most in this protest
was the date and the signature. "On board the
Bellerophon, at sea. Napoleon." "These are the
harmonies of immensity," says the prose-poet.

In going out of Plymouth the *Bellerophon* had first
steered east with a stern breeze. Presently it drew
closer to the wind, hugging the shore and cruising

about. The passengers did not understand the object of these manœuvres.

Saturday, August 5. This day went by in the same manner as the previous one.

Sunday, August 6. Toward noon the *Bellerophon* anchored in the roadstead of Start Point, where it was not in safety, whereas in that of Torbay, which was very near, it would have been excellently placed. It was very soon evident why it did not go to Torbay. At Start Point they were about to be joined by the *Northumberland*, which was to convey Napoleon to Saint Helena. A few instants later this vessel appeared, and also two frigates crowded with troops destined to garrison the island. The ship *Thunderer* also came up, on which was floating the ensign of Lord Keith, the chief admiral of the naval station. During the day Lord Keith and Sir George Cockburn came aboard the *Bellerophon* and remitted to the Emperor a copy of the instructions they had received. These enjoined that on the following day Napoleon and the members of his suite should be disarmed, their baggage searched, and their money seized and held in trust.

The Emperor had only three hundred and fifty thousand francs in gold, and the diamond necklace which Queen Hortense had forced him to accept when he left Malmaison. The necklace was intrusted to Las Cases, who concealed it about his person. As to the gold, it was divided among the domestics, who hid it in their clothing, with the exception of eighty thousand francs, which sum was all that was seized on by the custom house agent. Napoleon selected Bertrand, Las Cases, and Montholon to accompany him. Gourgaud, in despair at being left behind, negotiated and succeeded. The instructions of the Admiralty did not permit the Emperor to take more than three officers. It was agreed to consider Las Cases a civilian, and, thanks to this interpretation, Gourgaud was admitted as a fourth person. As to his sword, Napoleon swore to himself that if they wished to take it from him, they would have to tear it away by force.

Monday, August 7. The moment for quitting the *Bellerophon* arrived. Toward eleven in the morning Lord Keith came in his long-boat. At one o'clock Napoleon made known that he was ready; Lord Keith's long-boat, which was to take him aboard the *Northumberland,* was waiting for him. He embraced the Duke of Rovigo, who, all in tears, threw himself at his feet and kissed his hands. He embraced General Lallemand also: "Be happy, my friends," he said to them. "We shall never see each other again, but my thoughts will never leave you nor any of those who have served me. Tell France that I pray for her." When he crossed the quarter-deck of the *Bellerophon,* the soldiers presented arms during three rolls of the drum. His step was firm and measured. He bade a polite and even friendly farewell to Captain Maitland, who was as greatly moved as if he had been French. "People may be astonished," said this brave seaman afterwards, "that there still remained an English officer prepossessed in favor of a man who had wrought so much harm to England. But Napoleon possessed the art of pleasing in such a high degree, that there are very few persons who, if, like me, they had been seated at his table almost a month, would not have experienced a sentiment of pity, and even of regret, in beholding a man endowed with such alluring qualities, and who had occupied such an elevated station in the world, reduced to the condition in which I saw him."

Calm, and full of dignity, the Emperor, on his way to the boat which was to take him to the *Northumberland*, bowed graciously to all who surrounded him. Those among the French who had obtained leave to follow him to Saint Helena seemed proud and happy; the others melted into tears. Las Cases said at this moment to Lord Keith: "You will observe, my Lord, that those who weep are those who are left behind."

XV.

A T the moment when the Emperor was about to leave the *Bellerophon* for the *Northumberland*, Admiral Keith said to him, with sorrowful respect, " General, England orders me to demand your sword." To this demand Napoleon responded by a glance so haughty that the Admiral dared not insist. The giant of battles kept his glorious sword. He was received on the *Northumberland* with the same honors as had been paid him on quitting the *Bellerophon*. The following day, August 8, 1815, the day of his departure for Saint Helena, he embraced once more those of his companions in misfortune who had not obtained authorization to follow him into captivity, but who were permitted to come and pay him their last homage on board the *Northumberland*. Among the number was Savary. The Emperor specially charged him to say to Captain Maitland that he had desired to give him some token of remembrance, and regretted having been rendered unable to do so ; for the rest, he felt no resentment toward him on account of what had occurred, because that was a matter which lay beyond his power. "I do not believe," he added, "that the Captain knowingly deceived me. On the contrary, I have seen in him so many evidences of honorable feeling as to persuade me that he is particularly grieved that the confidence I placed in his flag became the snare of my ill-fortune, and that he was made the instrument of a most shameful infraction of honor and morality and every law respected by the least uncivilized nations."

Shortly afterwards, while the *Bellerophon* and the *Thunderer* sailed for Plymouth, the *Northumberland* got under way for Saint Helena, which it was not to reach until October 15. When the vessel passed the heights of the Cape of La Hogue, Napoleon recognized the coasts of France. He saluted them, extending his hands toward the shore, and crying, with a voice full of emotion: "Adieu, land of heroes! Adieu, dear France! A few less traitors, and you would be the mistress of the world!"

The English were about to put the captive upon a gigantic pedestal. Without knowing it, and in spite of themselves, those who tortured him were to become the courtiers of his glory. The rock of Saint Helena, as serviceable to his memory as the prison of the Conciergerie was to that of Marie Antoinette, was far preferable to the hospitality he might have received in this or that English palace. The author of the *Génie du Christianisme* had reason for saying: "What rôle could the fugitive, perhaps also fêted, have played beside the Thames, in sight of France invaded, and Wellington dictator in the Louvre? The high destiny of Napoleon served him better. The English, in allowing themselves to be carried away by a narrow and bitter policy, failed of their final triumph. Instead of ruining their suppliant by throwing open to him their prisons or their banquets, they made the crown they had torn away more brilliant than ever in the eyes of posterity. He grew greater in his captivity on account of the immense terror of the Powers. In vain did the ocean enchain him; armed Europe encamped upon the shore, its eyes fastened on the sea."

Is it not remarkable to see Chateaubriand, the author of *Buonaparte et les Bourbons*, that brochure which was worth more than an army to Louis XVIII., thus making admiration succeed to anger, and coming back at various times to the same reflection? "The Emperor," he says again, "made a mistake in the interests of his memory when he desired to remain in Europe. There he could have been nothing but a prisoner, vulgar or dishonored. His old part was played out; but, that part ended, a new position prepared for him a new renown. No man who has made a universal fame has had an end equal to that of Napoleon. He cannot be called, as he was after his first downfall, the autocrat of certain iron and marble quarries, of which these might furnish him a statue and those a sword. An eagle, they gave him a rock, on whose point he stood, sunbeaten, until his death, and from whence he was seen by all the earth."

During the voyage the Emperor was calm, resigned, and showed the most exquisite politeness to all his attendants and to the English. The latter refused him the titles of Šire, Emperor, or Majesty. They addressed him as General or Your Excellency.

Las Cases thus describes the interior of the ship: " The space behind the mizzen mast contained two common and two private cabins. The first of the two former was the dining-room, about ten feet wide, and the whole width of the vessel in length; it was lighted by a porthole at each end and a large sky-light. The saloon occupied all the room remaining after two cabins, exactly similar to each other, had been cut off from it to left and right. Each of these had one door into the dining-room and another into the saloon. The Emperor occupied the left-hand one, where his campaign bed had been set up; the Admiral had the other. It had been strictly provided that the saloon should be common and not given to the Emperor for his private use: the Ministers were anxiously afraid of even so trifling a deference."

And here is the description of the dining-table, which followed the shape of the cabin: " The Emperor sat with his back to the saloon, facing toward the bow of the vessel; on his left was Madame Bertrand, on his right the Admiral; on the right of the Admiral sat Madame de Montholon. The table turned at this point. On the short side the commander of the vessel, Captain Ross, was seated, and opposite to him, on the corresponding side, M. de Montholon beside Madame Bertrand; then came the purser. The side opposite the Emperor, beginning at the captain of the ship, was occupied by the Grand Marshal, the General, the Colonel of the 53d, myself, and Baron Gourgaud. Every day the Admiral invited one or two officers, who sat between us. I was almost opposite the Emperor. The band of the 53d, which had been but recently recruited, played during the whole dinner time, much to our annoyance."

The English have the habit of sitting a long time at table, after dessert, to drink and chat. The Emperor, who detested long meals, could not conform to this custom. From the first day, he rose at once after the coffee and went out on the bridge. As Sir George Cockburn appeared to be somewhat astonished at this, Madame Bertrand said to him, " Do not forget, Admiral, that you are dealing with one who has been master of the world, and to whose table kings begged the honor of being admitted." " That is true," returned the Admiral, who was a courteous and well-bred man. After that he abridged the length of the courses, and caused coffee to be served before the usual time to the Emperor and those who went out with him. Napoleon left the table as soon as he finished eating. The English rose and remained standing until he left the dining-saloon, and then sat down again to chat and drink for another hour.

The Emperor walked on the bridge until nightfall; afterwards he re-entered the saloon, where he played cards for half an hour, and then retired.

"Napoleon's fête, which was also his birthday, came round during the voyage," says Walter Scott. "It was the fifteenth of August, a day for which the Pope had expressly canonized a Saint Napoleon to be the Emperor's patron. And now, strange revolution! he was celebrating his fête on board an English man-of-war, which was conveying him to the place of his exile, which was also to be the place of his tomb. Yet Napoleon appeared gay and contented throughout the voyage, and saw with pleasure that he was successful at cards, which seemed to him a good omen." In the morning all his companions in misfortune, having asked permission to enter his cabin, came in together. "The Emperor could not guess the reason," says Las Cases. "It was his fête, but he had not thought of it. We had been accustomed on this anniversary to see him in larger places, replenished with the tokens of his power; but we had never brought him more sincere good wishes, nor hearts more full of him."

The next day, August 16, they doubled Cape Finisterre; on the 18th, Cape Saint Vincent; on the 19th, they passed across the Straits of Gibraltar. On the succeeding days they sailed along the coast of Africa towards Madeira. On the 27th, they passed the Canaries, and on the 29th, crossed the tropic. On September 1, they passed the Islands of Cape Verde.

The days followed one another, sad and monoto-
nous. The heat was oppressive, and the sea often
rough. Napoleon slept badly. He rose often in the
night, seeking a refuge from insomnia and grief in
reading. Shut up in his cabin, he spent his mornings in reading or writing, and his evenings in walking on the bridge. He used often to go and lean
against the next to last cannon on the left side of the
vessel, near the gangway. Presently the whole crew
were calling it the Emperor's cannon. Chatting
with this or that one of his attendants in misfortune,
he passed in review the places of his existence, at once
bizarre and grandiose, which had in it something of
legend, romance, and tragedy. Frequently his companions, transported by the eloquence of these re-
citals, which, like his soul, were full of fire, begged
him to dictate what he had told so well. "No, no,"
he responded, as if sick of his own story; "let history manage as best it can! It may search out the
truth if it wants to know it. The archives of State
are full of it. France will find there the monuments
of her glory, and, if she prizes them, let her busy herself in preserving them from oblivion." Then, remembering his most famous victories: "They are
granite," said he. "The tooth of envy can do nothing
with them." Las Cases, by calling his attention to
the monotony of the hours, and the necessity of whil-
ing away their dulness by work, at last induced him,
on September 9, to dictate something about the siege
of Toulon. Afterwards he dictated his recollections
of the first Italian campaign.

On September 23, they crossed the Line, by zero of latitude, zero of longitude, and zero of declination; "a circumstance," says Las Cases, "which chance might not renew in a century, since it is necessary to arrive precisely at the first meridian toward noon, to pass the Line at the same hour, and to arrive there at the same time as the sun. This was a day of great mirth and much disorder for the whole crew; it was the ceremony which our sailors call the baptism, and the English, the big shaving day. The sailors, arrayed in the most ridiculous costumes, conduct, with great ceremony, all those who have never crossed the Line to the feet of one of their number who personates Neptune. There one's beard is drenched with bilge water and shaved off with an immense razor. Pails of water thrown over you from all sides, and the rude laughter with which the crew accompany your flight, complete your initiation into the grand mysteries. Nobody escapes; even the officers are in some ways more badly used than the least of the sailors. We alone, by a perfect courtesy on the part of the Admiral, who, until then, had amused himself by making us dread this terrible ceremony, escaped its inconveniences and its ridicule. We were conducted, with every attention and respect, to the feet of the clumsy god, from whom each of us received a characteristic compliment: this was the extent of our trials. The Emperor was scrupulously respected throughout this saturnalia, which usually respects nothing and nobody. Having been apprised of the ordinary custom and the deference displayed towards him, he ordered a hundred napoleons to be distributed to the grotesque Neptune and his attendants, but this the Admiral refused to concede, as much out of prudence as politeness."

Apropos of this journey, Chateaubriand has said in his *Mémoires d'outre-tombe:* " The sea which Napoleon crossed was not that friendly sea which had borne him from the harbors of Corsica, the sands of Aboukir, and the rocks of Elba to the shores of Provence: it was that inimical ocean which, having hemmed him in in Germany, France, Portugal, and Spain, never opened before save to close in upon him from behind. It is probable that in feeling the waves impel his vessel, and the trade winds with their constant breathing blow him further on, he did not make the same reflections on his catastrophe which it inspires in me. Every man feels his life in his own way; he who gives the world a grand spectacle is less touched and instructed by it than the spectator. Occupied with the past as if it might revive again, hoping still in the midst of his recollections, Bonaparte hardly noticed that he was crossing the Line: he did not ask what hand had traced the circles in which the spheres are constrained to imprison their eternal march."

However, the end of the voyage was approaching. Since the Emperor had begun to spend his mornings in dictation, of which he daily grew more fond, the hours had been less heavy to him. According to

Las Cases, he would begin by seeming to distrust himself, saying that he would never be able to accomplish anything. Then he would ponder for some minutes; then, rising and walking back and forth, he would begin to dictate. From that moment he was another man. Everything flowed straight from the source; he spoke as if by inspiration: expressions, places, dates, nothing retarded him.

At last, on Sunday, October 15, seventy days after leaving England, and one hundred and ten after leaving Paris, Napoleon perceived the Island of Saint Helena, which was to be his grave. He thought then of Corsica, which had been his cradle. Victor Hugo has said: —

> " These isles, where the surges pound
> Between the naked reefs,
> Are like two vessels of prey
> Chained to an eternal anchor.
> The hand that fixed the savage sites
> Of these black shores,
> And willed to cover them with dread,
> Made them so terrible, perhaps,
> That Bonaparte might there be born,
> And here Napoleon might die."

But listen to Chateaubriand: —

" On October 15, the *Northumberland* had reached the height of Saint Helena. The passenger went on the bridge; it was with difficulty that he descried an almost imperceptible black spot in the azure immensity; he took a spyglass; he observed this grain of earth as he had in other days observed a fortress in the middle of a lake. He saw the village of Saint James, closed in by precipitous rocks; not a wrinkle in that sterile face in which a cannon was not hanging. It seemed as if the captive were to be received according to his own genius."

The anchor was lowered toward midday. It touched bottom. In contemplating this island, the result of a volcanic eruption, which cast it into the middle of the ocean, with its inaccessible coasts and arid rocks, lifting their black crests to heaven, and dominated by the peak of Diana, which overlooks them all, Napoleon remained impassible. No one could surprise upon his countenance even the faintest trace of expression. Perhaps he understood that such a prison was worthy of a Titan thunder-stricken. In reality, he was not a subject for self-pity. As M. Veuillot has said: "Five years were to be accorded him to behold himself in the past and in the future, to justify or explain himself before men, to humble himself before God. During five years he remains upright on the threshold of the tomb; he descends into it step by step, surrounded by admiration, love, and pity, consecrated by expiation as he had been by glory."

We lost sight long ago of the heroine of this study, Marie Louise. Was it not the fault of the faithless Empress, who, in this grandiose and terrible drama of the Hundred Days, and the second death-struggle of the Empire, never once lifted her voice to plead the cause of her husband and her son? Not a letter;

NAPOLEON AT ST. HELENA

not a line; not a phrase to console the vanquished of Waterloo, the captive of the *Bellerophon*. The English themselves were moved to pity. Marie Louise remained cold. Not a tear; not a movement of compassion; well-being preferred to duty; mean calculations repelling magnanimous inspirations; not one of those generous accents which from century to century would have re-echoed in the ears of posterity!

One is still more inclined to severity toward the former Regent of the Empire, the wife of Napoleon, and the mother of the King of Rome, when reading these two letters addressed to her by Prince Metternich: —

"Paris, July 18, 1815. MADAME: I promised, before my departure from Vienna, to inform Your Imperial Majesty directly of whatever related to Napoleon's fate. You will see by the inclosed extract from the *Moniteur* that he has surrendered himself to the English vessel, the *Bellerophon*, after having vainly attempted to escape the vigilance of the cruisers in front of Rochefort. According to an arrangement made between the Powers, he will be imprisoned at Fort Saint George, in the north of Scotland, under the surveillance of Austrian, Prussian, French, and Russian commissioners. He will be very well treated, and given all the liberty compatible with the completest certainty that he cannot escape."

"August 13, 1815. MADAME: Napoleon is on board the *Northumberland*, on his way to Saint

Helena. The only news we have of his departure
from Torbay comes by telegraph; but we know that
it was out at sea that he left one vessel for the other.
He was sent away on the *Bellerophon* because the
crowd of sightseers increased so greatly about the
vessel, that there was no certainty that there would
not be a scandal."

What dryness in these letters! Not a word of
pity for such a memorable misfortune! Metternich
still addresses Marie Louise as Imperial Majesty,
while he calls the Emperor simply Napoleon. At
least he might have said, "your husband," to the
former Empress. Assuredly the astute Minister, the
most skilful of courtiers, must have been very certain
of her forgetfulness when he spoke to her of her
husband in terms so laconic, so disdainful! The
Austrian statesman knew very well that instead of
desiring to be the companion of a captive, she had
but one thought, — that of reigning at Parma, with
General Neipperg as a morganatic prince-consort.
The letters of the Minister of the Emperor Francis,
coming after Napoleon's departure for Saint Helena,
suggest painful reflections. It was here, then, that
the marriage so much celebrated, so much exalted,
which it was supposed would procure the happiness
of Napoleon, the glory of France, and the repose and
prosperity of the world, was to end!

Marie Louise did not even suspect the interest she
still inspired in the last faithful adherents of the
Napoleonic cause. Baron de Bausset, formerly pre-

fect of the imperial palace, the only Frenchman who
still remained near her, repeats the conversations he
had at this time with a Polish count who had fought
under Napoleon's standard, and who never spoke of
the former Empress but as "my general's widow."
She was a widow, in fact; a widow during her husband's lifetime! "So many confused ideas take possession of me," said the brave officer, "when I see
her alone and pensive on her balcony, that I am
tempted to weep, I have at once so much pleasure
and so much pain in looking at her. There are days
when, unable to resist my desire to see her son, I
have myself driven out to Schoenbrunn. I have had
the happiness of seeing him walking with his governor in the gardens of the palace, attended by a
single footman. What beautiful fair hair! . . . I
looked at him well. . . . His eyes seem bluer than
his father's. In the upper part of his face he has the
features and the forehead of Napoleon; the others
recall his mother. Alas! I said to myself in looking
at him, if that fatal Russian campaign had not been
undertaken, what a brilliant destiny would have been
reserved for this young child who now, separated
from his father, is obliged to grow up in a strange
land. . . . And we Poles, so frankly devoted and
loyal to France, would not have been divided between
three rival crowns, between whom and ourselves
there exists no tie of habit or manners."

To this recital Baron de Bausset adds: "I have no
longer any answer to make to the Polish count; but

he overwhelmed me, nevertheless, with a multitude
of questions. Only, when he asked me what impression the latest tidings had made upon the heart of
Marie Louise, I replied that the story of so many
misfortunes had been told her by the Austrian Empress, who seemed reserved for this sort of communi-
cations. This princess had come eagerly to Marie
Louise. Their private interview lasted until it was
time to sit down at table. The mother-in-law had
a very marked appearance of satisfaction. On the
features of Marie Louise I perceived an emotion she
was trying to subdue. I sat opposite their Majesties,
and lost not an expression of their faces."

This emotion which Marie Louise sought vainly to
conceal, is the attenuating circumstance we plead in
her favor. Were not the politicians who surrounded
the poor young wife with so many snares, and labored
so systematically to turn her from her duties and cor-
rupt her, the real criminals? Left to herself, — let
us render her this justice, — she would have played a
wholly different part. They abused her youth, her
feebleness. That is why, less severe than posterity,
her husband pardoned her. On the rock of Saint
Helena he had not a single word of bitterness, a
single word of reproach for the faithless one. And,
at the beginning of his testament he thus invokes
those three great souvenirs, — Religion, Country, and
Marie Louise: —

"April 15, 1821. At Longwood, Island of Saint
Helena. 1. I die in the Apostolic and Roman relig-

ion, in whose bosom I was born more than fifty years ago; 2. I desire that my ashes may repose beside the Seine, in the midst of that French people I have so much loved; 3. I have always been satisfied with my dearest wife, Marie Louise; I have preserved to the last moment the tenderest sentiments toward her; I pray her to be careful to secure my son from the snares which still surround his childhood."

Alas! why was not Marie Louise more worthy of this eulogy of the prisoner? Why had he not the right to say of her what he had said of his brother Jerome's wife: "The Princess Catherine of Würtemberg has written her name in history with her own hands." There was a devoted, disinterested, courageous spouse, the true model of wives and mothers! When, in 1814, every inducement, every possible effort, was made to divorce her, so as to marry her to some rich and powerful prince, some sovereign possibly, she wrote to her father, the King of Würtemberg: "Forced by political reasons to espouse the King, my husband, fate willed that I should find myself the happiest woman in existence. I bear towards my husband all sentiments united — love, tenderness, esteem. In this painful moment, would the best of fathers destroy my internal happiness, the sole happiness, indeed, which remains to me?" And the noble Princess loved exile and poverty with her husband better than native land and wealth without him.

This difference between the conduct of Catherine of Würtemberg and that of Marie Louise is easily explained. It must be admitted, women never push devotion and charity to heroism except when they have love for a motive — love human or divine, the love of the lover for her well-beloved, of the wife for her husband, of the mother for her child, of the Christian for her God. Then the feeble sex becomes strong. Then are realized those grand words of the *Imitation of Jesus Christ:* " Love is capable of all; it accomplishes many things which exhaust those who do not love. Love watches always, and even in slumber does not sleep. No fatigue wearies it; no fear troubles it; but, like a living and ardent flame, it always ascends on high and opens a sure passage through every obstacle." Why was one of these princesses sublime, and the other vulgar? For a very simple reason : Catherine of Würtemberg was in love with Jerome; Marie Louise was not in love with Napoleon.

INDEX.

Aix in Savoy, Marie Louise takes the baths at, 31 *et seq.*

Alexander I.; magnanimity of, to Napoleon, 5; caricature of, 54; interest of, in Marie Louise, 73; intimacy of, with Eugene de Beauharnais, 74; his sympathy with Marie Louise, 75; his ill luck at the Princess Esterhazy's lottery, 79; indignation of, at the secret treaty against him, 127; under the spell of Madame de Krudener, 127; opposes the suppression of the tricolored flag, 128; his antipathy to the Bourbons, 129; conversation of, on the situation of France, 130; willing to establish Marie Louise as Regent, 130; favors the Duke of Orleans, 131.

Arndt, Maurice, his *Catechism for German Soldiers and Military Men*, 114 *et seq.*

Arrighi, Vicar-General of Elba, issues his charge respecting Napoleon, 16.

Azores, Talleyrand proposes to remove Napoleon to, 80, 82.

Bassano, Duke of, urges Napoleon to seize the reins of government, 202.

Bausset, Baron de, interview of, with a Polish count, 293.

Beauharnais, Eugene de, intimacy of, with Alexander I., 74.

Beker, General, sent by the Minister of War to take charge of Napoleon, 204; his magnanimous loyalty, 205; takes Napoleon's proposal to attack the Allies, to the Provisional Government, 211.

Bellangé, Hippolyte, his painting of the agony of the Guard, 169.

Bellerophon, the, takes Napoleon to England, 241; goes to Plymouth, 242; transfers Napoleon to the *Northumberland* at Start Point, 257.

Bertrand, General, describes Napoleon's journey to Elba, 6.

Bertrand, Madame, tries to throw herself overboard, 253.

Bonaparte, Joseph, meets Marie Louise at Sécheron, 32.

Bonaparte, Lucien, recalled by Napoleon, 142; describes the conduct of the Assembly after Waterloo, 177; dialogue of, with Napoleon, 181; addresses the Chambers, 183 *et seq.*; on the abdication, 188; takes the oath to Napoleon II., 192; avows the loss of the imperial cause, 192.

Bourmont, General de, and other officers go over to the enemy before Waterloo, 157.

Brignole, Countess of, lady of honor to Marie Louise, 5; implores Marie Louise to rejoin Napoleon, 132.

Bunbury, Sir Henry, reads to Napoleon the decision of the British Government as to his exile, 248.

Caffarelli, Madame, her recollections of Napoleon at Malmaison, 201.

Carnot, named by Napoleon Minister of the Interior, 104; supports the idea of a dictatorship for Napoleon after Waterloo, 176.

Caroline Murat, Queen of Naples, 25.

Caroline, Princess of Wales, character of, 48; has an interview with Marie Louise, 49.

Castlereagh, Lord, rudeness of, to Marie Louise, 75.

Chateaubriand, reflections of, on hearing the cannonading of Waterloo, 162; quoted, 193, 256, 261, 262, 268, 269.

Constant, Benjamin, tergiversation of, 108.

Dalesme, General, delivers the command of Elba to Napoleon, 12; proclamation of, to the Elbans, 12.

Declaration of March 13, a medley of hate and terror, 113.

Decrés, Duke, makes every effort to save Napoleon from captivity, 207.

Domon, General, sent by Napoleon to make a reconnoissance, 163; reports that Blücher is coming up instead of Grouchy, 164.

Drouot, General, receives from General Dalesme the command of Elba, 12.

Elba, Francis I. objects to, as a place of exile for Napoleon, 4; Napoleon takes possession of, 14; Napoleon's return from, announced in Vienna, 79; the embarkation, etc., 82.

England, opposition in, to the attitude of the Ministry towards France, 126; Napoleon seeks an asylum in, 224.

Esterhazy, Princess Paul, gems worn by, 58; lottery at the house of, 79.

Etruria, the King of, at Paris, 57; the Queen of, disputes the possession of Parma with Marie Louise, 57.

Exelmans, General, declares resistance useless and the Tuileries is opened to Napoleon, 102.

"Field of May," the ceremony of, 143, 145.

Fouché, his contradictory orders as to Napoleon's departure, 206.

Francis II., his adroit alienation of his daughter from Napoleon, 2; letter of, to Napoleon, concerning Marie Louise, 3; to Metternich, respecting Napoleon's place of exile, 4; has no longer sympathy for him, 5; refuses to recognize his daughter as a sovereign, 23.

Gourgaud, General, permitted to accompany Napoleon, 258.

Grenoble, gates of, forced by Napoleon's soldiers, 96.

Grouchy goes to Wavres instead of to Waterloo, 164; fails to arrive, 166; safe at Laon, 186.

Guard, Old, Napoleon's, lands at Elba, 18; detachment of, at Elba, accompanies Napoleon on his return, 85; charges at Waterloo and covers the retreat, 167.

Hortense, Queen, insists on Napoleon's accepting her diamond necklace, 213.

Hotham, Admiral, visits Napoleon on the *Bellerophon*, 238.

Inconstant, the, Napoleon's return from Elba in, 83.

Jaucourt, M. de, letter of, to Talleyrand, on the situation of France, 126.

Josephine, Napoleon recalls his life with, at Malmaison, 201.

Jung, Colonel, quoted, 107.

Keith, Admiral, demands Napoleon's sword, 260.

Krudener, Madame de, her fatal influence over Alexander I., 127.

Labédoyère, General de, carries his regiment over to Napoleon, 95; speaks hotly against those who refuse to recognize Napoleon II., 193; excluded by the government of Louis XVIII. from amnesty, 252.

La Bruyère, quotation from, 54.

Lafayette, describes Napoleon's appearance, 152; discourse of, in the Chamber after Waterloo, 178; sends word to Napoleon that he must abdicate at once or be deposed, 186.

Laon, the news of Napoleon's abdication reaches the soldiers at, 198.

Las Cases, Count de, quoted, 219; agitation of, on hearing that Napoleon was to be sent to Saint Helena, 243; describes the thronging of the people to view Napoleon at Plymouth, 245; chosen by Napoleon to accompany him to Saint Helena, 253; describes the interior of the *Northumberland*, 263.

Las Cases, Countess de, meets her husband at Malmaison, 202.

La Tour-du-Pin, Baron de, his account of the death and funeral of Queen Marie Caroline, 29; letters of, concerning Marie Louise at the Vienna Congress, 55; concerning the tournament, 59, 60; concerning Count Neipperg, 63; regarding the "Little Bonaparte," 66.

Lavalette makes a way for Napoleon to enter the Tuileries, 103.

Ligne, Prince de, interest of in Napoleon's son, 69.

Ligny, battle of, gained by Napoleon, 157.

Louis XVI., mass of expiation offered for at Vienna, 71.

Louis XVIII., address of, to the Chambers before his flight, 99; takes flight, 100.

Maitland, Captain, receives Napoleon's envoys, 224; his courtesy to the French officers sent by Napoleon, 226; declares his intentions with regard to the French frigates, 227; advises Napoleon's taking refuge in England, 228, 232; emotion of, at Napoleon's departure from the *Bellerophon*, 258.

Manuel, proclaims Napoleon II. as nominal sovereign, 196.

Marie Caroline, Queen of the Two Sicilies, her history and traits, 24 *et seq.*; her adventurous journey to Vienna, 26; urges Marie Louise to rejoin Napoleon, 27; death of, 29.

Marie Louise, her gradual transformation, 1; leaves France, 5, 11; her suite and journey, 5 *et seq.*; expenses of, 6; her regret at not having met her husband at Fontainebleau, 6; her solicitude for Napoleon, 7; her final separation from him decided by the Austrian Government, 8; arrives at Schoenbrunn, 10; her life there, 22; her sisters, 22; visited by Queen Marie Caroline, 27; goes to Aix in Savoy, as the Countess of Colerno, 32; met and escorted by General Count Neipperg, 33; surrounded by Imperialists and still true to Napoleon, 34; her correspondence with Méneval, 35; the French Government uneasy about her, 40; in Switzerland with Neipperg, 42, 46; at Braunau, 52; not present at the fêtes of the Vienna Congress, 55; attends the rehearsal of the tournament, 58; visits the Russian Empress, 62; removes the French imperial arms from her liveries, 62; begins to love Count Neipperg, 63; holds no communication with Napoleon without her father's consent, 65; her ambition to be Duchess of Parma, 72; sympathy of Alexander I. with, 75; the stipulations of the Fontainebleau treaty with respect to her, disregarded, 75; refuses to be content with Lucca, 77; consents not to take her son there, 77; hears of Napoleon's quitting Elba, 111 ; her struggle with regard to joining Napoleon, 112; causes Count Neipperg to write to Metternich that she had no part in Napoleon's projects, 116; enthralled by General Neipperg, 120; declares to Méneval that she will not return to France, 124; the results of her decision, 125; Alexander I. willing to establish her as Regent, 130; her indifference to Napoleon, 131; her constant intimacy with General Neipperg, 133; her lack of regret for the death of General Neipperg's wife, 134; her strange affection for him, 134; persists in her refusal to go to France, 135; gives up her son, 136; bids Méneval adieu, and declares a separation from Napoleon a necessity, 137; letters of Metternich to, on Napoleon's fate, 271; her sentiments towards Napoleon devoid of love, 276.

Méneval, Baron de, in the suite of Marie Louise, 6; letter of, concerning Marie Louise at Vienna, 66; on the hostility at Vienna to Marie Louise and her son, 67; conversation of, with Marie Louise, concerning her course, 124; his journal kept at Schoenbrunn, 133; his last interview with Marie Louise, 135, 137; takes leave of Napoleon's son, 136; gives Napoleon news of his wife's decision and of his son,

138; describes his demeanor, 140.

Meurthe, Boulay de la, asserts that by Napoleon's abdication, his son reigns in due course, 195.

Michel, Colonel, brings to Paris the news of Waterloo, 174.

Michelet, quoted, 200.

Military fête given in the Champ-de-Mars by the Imperial Guard, 106.

Moniteur Universel, account in, of a grand rout in Vienna during the Congress, 61; the proclamation of Napoleon in, before Waterloo, 172.

Montebello, Countess of, in the suite of Marie Louise, 5.

Montesquiou, Countess of, governess of the King of Rome, 2, 5, 65; deprived of the care of Napoleon's son, 117; not allowed to return to France, 132.

Montrond, M. de, sent to Vienna to endeavor to recall Marie Louise to her husband, 120; his interview with Talleyrand and others, 121 *et seq.;* brings to Napoleon letters and the details of his mission, 123.

Murat, reconciled to Napoleon by the Princess Borghese, 119; beaten at Tolentino, 134, 144; proclamation of, at Rimini, 143; exiled to Provence, 144.

Musset, Alfred de, quoted, 9.

Naples surrendered to the English and Austrians by Madame Murat, 144.

Napoleon supposes Francis I. is interested in his fate, 5; arrives at Elba, 11; ceremony of embarkation, 13; official report of his taking possession of the island, 14; visits the public institutions, 15; forms his court and receives his subjects, 17; his army, 18; happy at Elba, 20; unwilling to have Marie Louise go to Aix, 31; visited by the Countess Walewska, 43; letter of, to the Grand Duke of Tuscany, enclosing one for Marie Louise, 64; the return of, from Elba, announced in Vienna, 79; the embarkation, 83; incidents of the voyage, 83 *et seq.*; his proclamations to the French people and the army, 85 *et seq.*; lands in the Bay of Juan, 87; takes his route for Paris, 88 *et seq.*; meets the Royalist Guard and receives their allegiance, 94 *et seq.*; at Grenoble, 97; writes to Marie Louise asking her to rejoin him, 97; enters Lyons in triumph, 98; meets Ney at Auxerre, 100; arrives at Fontainebleau, 101; enters the Tuileries, 103; reviews the soldiers and names Carnot Minister of the Interior, 104; visits Saint Denis, 106; grand fête in his honor in the Champ-de-Mars, 106; finds the evidences of general tergiversation, 108; strives to regain possession of his wife and son, 116; sends letters to Vienna to this end, 116; sends de Montrond to Vienna to recall Marie Louise to him, 120; receives from Méneval the intelligence of his wife's decision and of the fate of his son, 139; no longer entertains any illusions, 140; recalls Lucien, 142; his propensity to sleep, 142; refuses to abdicate, 143; exiles Murat, 144; celebrates the inauguration of the liberal Empire in the "Field of May," 145; his speech, 148; addresses the National Guard, 149; at the Tuileries for the last time, 150; his discourse at the opening of the Chambers, 152; and to the Chamber of Peers, 153; his plans at Waterloo, 157; gains the battle of Ligny, 157;

physically and mentally fatigued, 159; fears that Wellington will retreat, 160; still has illusions, 160; gives the signal for battle to begin, 161; in doubt about the arrival of Grouchy, 163; sends re-enforcements to Ney, 165; hesitates and becomes perplexed, 166, sends the Guard to the attack, 167; gives the signal to retreat, 168; his own retreat, 170; in Paris again, 174; undecided and powerless, 175; asks for a temporary dictatorship from the Chambers, 176; wavers and feels himself vanquished, 179; dialogue of, with Lucien Bonaparte, 181; the common people and soldiers receive him with enthusiasm, 182; informed by Lucien that a *coup d'état* or an abdication are the only alternatives, 185; receives word from Lafayette that he must abdicate at once or be deposed, 186; abdicates in favor of his son, 188; his address to the deputation from the Assembly, 190; goes to Malmaison, 198; recalls his life there with Josephine, 201; delays his departure, 203; decree of the Provisional Government for the transportation of, to America, 204; misgivings of, as to the intentions of the Provisional Government, 205; Fouché urges that he should depart in disguise, 206; contradictory instructions from Fouché, 206; refuses to escape on a merchant vessel, 207; prepares to depart, but cherishes a lingering hope, 208; French frigates placed at his disposal, 210; proposes to General Beker to take command of the army again, 210; sends him to the Provisional Government with the proposal, 211; which is rejected, 211; leaves Malmaison with his attendants,

212; accepts a diamond necklace from Queen Hortense, 213; at Rambouillet, 214; still cherishes illusions, 216; is welcomed at Rochefort by the National Guards, 209; detained there by unfavorable winds and the English ships, 217; propositions made for his flight, 221; goes on board the *Saale*, 222; decides to confide himself to the generosity of England, 224; sends envoys to Captain Maitland of the *Bellerophon*, 224; orders the *Saale* to sail at once, 229; receives a visit from Joseph Bonaparte, 230; letter of, to the Prince Regent, 233; his instructions to General Gourgaud, 234; goes on board the *Bellerophon*, 237; his suite, 238; drills the soldiers on the *Bellerophon*, 239; breakfasts on the *Superb* with Admiral Hotham, 240; incidents of the voyage to England, 240; arrives at Torbay, 241; the *Bellerophon* ordered to Plymouth, 242; curiosity excited by his presence, 244; made acquainted with the decision to send him to Saint Helena, 247; his speech in reply, 248 *et seq.*; etiquette observed with, on the *Bellerophon*, 252; Las Cases combats the idea of suicide which he inclined to, 254; his written protest, 255; conceals his money and diamonds, 257; does not surrender his sword to Admiral Keith, 260; is transferred to the *Northumberland*, 260; his habits on shipboard, 264 *et seq.*; spends his mornings in dictation, 268; in sight of Saint Helena, 269; testament of, at Longwood, 274.

Napoleon II., Napoleon abdicates in his favor, 188; proclaimed Emperor by the Chamber of Deputies, 195; his reign a phantasm, 197; see King of Rome.

Neipperg, General Count, his character and career, 2; escorts Marie Louise into Aix, 33; closely attendant upon Marie Louise, 46; his success as the chamberlain of Marie Louise, 63; begins the war with Murat, 118, 120; his influence over Marie Louise, 133; defeats Murat, 134; death of his wife, 134.

Nettement, M. Alfred, quoted, 190, 251.

Ney, Marshal, declares for Napoleon, 99; meets him at Auxerre, 100; gives a banquet to the officers at Lille, 105; unsuccessful at Quatre-Bras, 157; attacks La Haye Sainte, 164; his intrepidity, 165; tries to meet death on the battle-field, 168; his despairing words before the Chamber of Peers, 191.

Northumberland, the, Napoleon transferred to, 260; description of, 263; crossing the line, 267.

Orleans, Duke of, Alexander I., in favor of a monarchy under, 128, 131.

Pacha de Surène, comedy played at the Vienna Congress, 60.

Philibert, Captain, of the *Saale* refuses to sail at Napoleon's orders, 229.

Poncé, Captain, of the *Méduse*, heroic proposition of, 229.

Provisional Government, decree of, as to Napoleon, 203; rejects Napoleon's proposal to attack the Allies, 211.

Rochefort, affection for Napoleon at, 217; port of, blockaded by English ships, 218.

Rome, King of, instructed to love and pray for his father, 2; no longer a king, 6; his melancholy and precocious ways, and instruction, 68; removed from the care of the Countess of Montesquiou, 117; see Napoleon II.

Royalists, the, in France, desire the success of the foreigner, 141.

Savary, General, excluded from amnesty by the government of Louis XVIII., 252.

Ségur, General de, will not recount the details of Napoleon's downfall, 156.

Schoenbrunn, fête at, 71.

Scott, Sir Walter, quoted, 207, 208; describes the concourse at Plymouth to view Napoleon, 246.

Soult, Marshal, his tergiversation, 108.

Talleyrand, Prince, letter to Metternich about Marie Louise's stay at Aix, 41; letter of, to Louis XVIII. upon the levity of Metternich, 59; desires to withhold Parma from Marie Louise, 73; letter of, respecting Alexander I., 74, 76 *et seq.*; describes the Lenten dissipations at Vienna, 78; obtains the signatures of the Powers to the declaration of March 13, 113; sends Louis XVIII. the *Warning to the Nations*, 114; writes to Louis XVIII. respecting de Montrond, 122; writes to Louis XVIII. explaining the hostility of Alexander I. to him, 129; reports a conversation of Alexander I. with Lord Clancarty, 129.

Tolentino, battle of, 134, 144; the "prologue to Waterloo," 144.

Torbay, the *Bellerophon* with Napoleon at, 241; commotion in the harbor of, 242.

Tournament during the Vienna Congress, 58.

Tyrol, the, restored to Austria, 9.

Vicenza, the Duke of, pleads Napoleon's cause for regaining possession of his wife and son, 116.

Victor Hugo, verses of, on Waterloo, 155.

Vienna Congress, entry of the sovereigns, 54; festivities of, 56.

"Vigil of Waterloo, The," 158.

Walewska, Countess, visits Napoleon at Elba, 43.

Warning to the Nations, the, 114.

Waterloo, Napoleon's plans before, 157; battle of, 161 *et seq.*; carnage after, 173.

Wellington's admiration of the charges of the French cuirassiers, 165; his sadness after Waterloo, 170.

Werner, fashionable preacher at Vienna, 70.

Würtemberg, Princess Catharine of, her fidelity to her husband, 275.